MEDIEVAL PERIOD AND THE RENAISSANCE

Edited by Tim Cooke

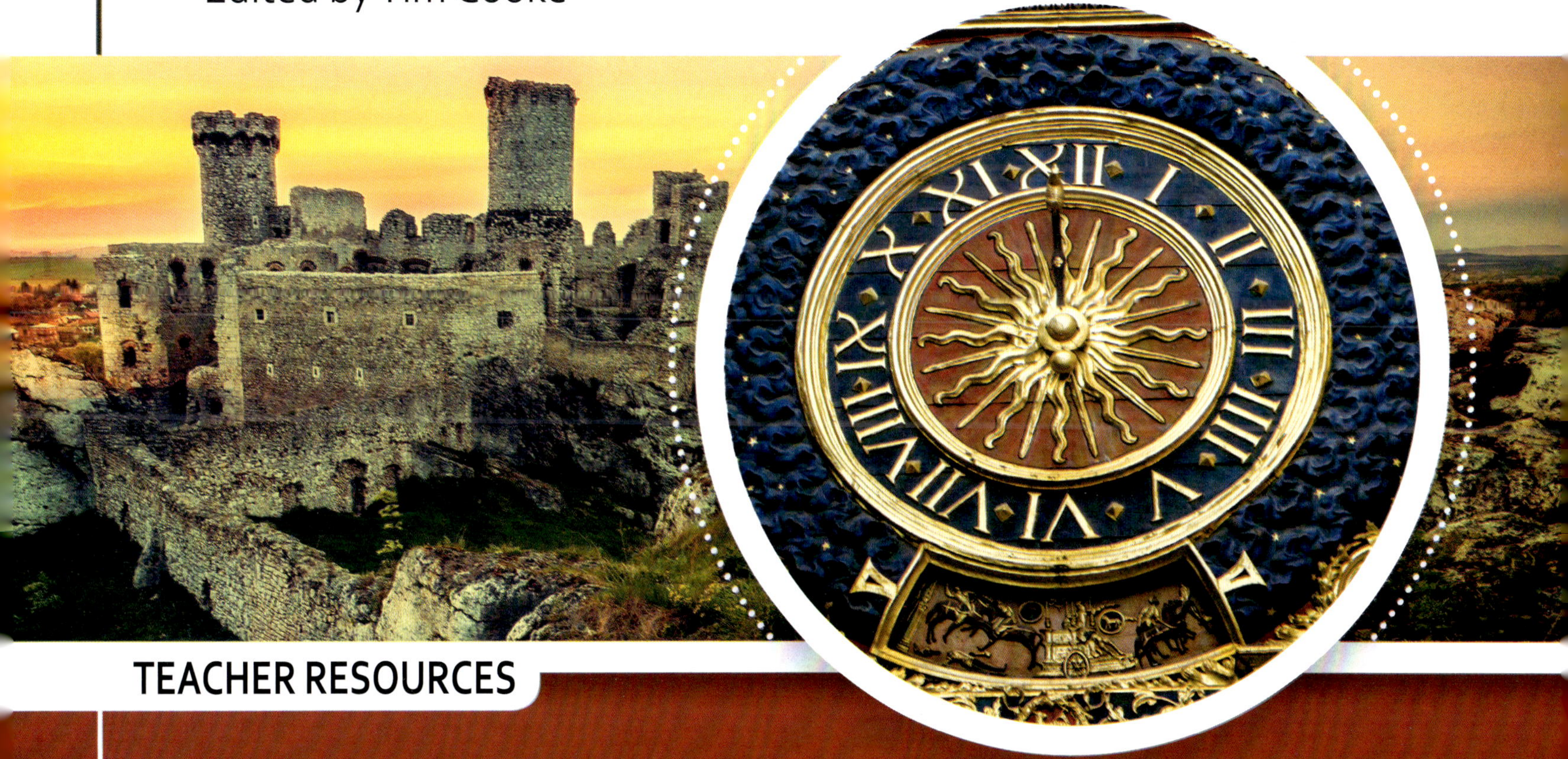

TEACHER RESOURCES

SCIENTIFIC DISCOVERY

LIGHTBOX
openlightbox.com

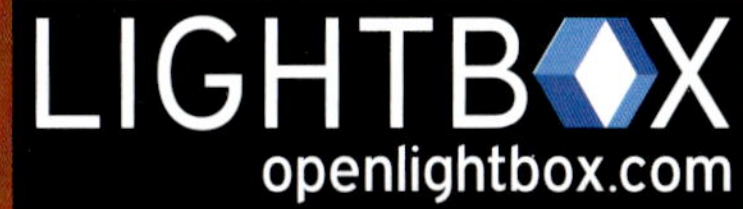

Lightbox is an all-inclusive digital solution for the teaching and learning of curriculum topics in an original, groundbreaking way. Lightbox is based on National Curriculum Standards.

STANDARD FEATURES OF LIGHTBOX

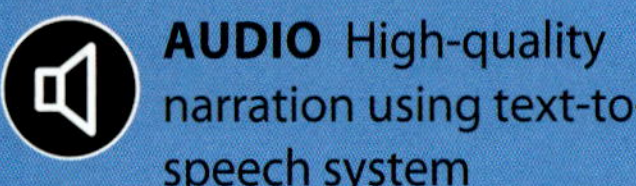
AUDIO High-quality narration using text-to-speech system

VIDEOS Embedded high-definition video clips

ACTIVITIES Printable PDFs that can be emailed and graded

WEBLINKS Curated links to external, child-safe resources

SLIDESHOWS Pictorial overviews of key concepts

TRANSPARENCIES Step-by-step layering of maps, diagrams, charts, and timelines

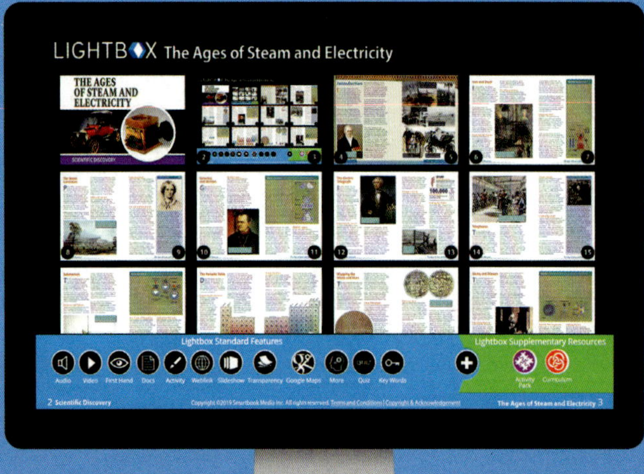

INTERACTIVE MAPS Interactive maps and aerial satellite imagery

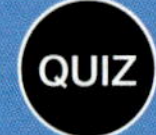
QUIZZES Ten multiple choice questions that are automatically graded and emailed for teacher assessment

KEY WORDS Matching key concepts to their definitions

MORE Extra information and details on the subject

FIRST HAND Letters, diaries, and other primary sources

DOCS Speeches, newspaper articles, and other historical documents

Contents

RUBRIC

Energy Project

Search online and in the library to identify three major sources of energy used throughout the Medieval and Renaissance worlds. Evaluate the importance of each one. An exemplary energy project will meet the following criteria:

- Each energy resource is listed as renewable or nonrenewable
- 3 or more advantages and disadvantages of the each energy resource are listed
- 3 or more uses of the energy resource are listed
- 4 to 5 specific facts about the energy resource are listed
- Conclusion of the project is a specific/detailed paragraph
- Research for the project is properly documented, all sources are credited

Introduction

The medieval period lasted for about a thousand years, from the fall of the Roman Empire in Europe in 476 until the 1400s, when the continent began a period of learning and exploration known as the Renaissance that continued until the 1600s. While the fall of the Roman Empire temporarily stalled the progress of European science, technology progressed in leaps and bounds. Europeans learned, for example, to harness wind power by the use of windmills. Ideas spread around the world, including from China. The **magnetic** compass and the discovery of how to make gunpowder were among the many Chinese inventions that found their way to Europe.

Early Muslim authors wrote encyclopedias about the use of plants in medicine.

Meanwhile, Arabian scientists preserved the discoveries of the past by collecting the work of earlier Greek and Asian scholars. They also made their own advances in many aspects of science. European scholars traveled widely in the Middle Ages, and some learned Arabic. In the 1100s, the English **philosopher** Adelard of Bath not only translated *Elements* by the ancient Greek mathematician Euclid, but also the astronomical tables of the ninth-century scholar Abu Jafar Muhammad ibn-Musa al-Khwarizmi, copying his use of Hindu-Arabic numerals. In 1145, the English scholar Robert of Chester made the first translation of al-Khwarizmi's *Hisab al-jabr w'al-muqabala*, "Calculation by Restoration and Reduction". This introduced the words "**algebra**" and "algorithm" to the English language.

Beginning in the fourteenth century in Italy, Renaissance scholars challenged almost all the intellectual approaches they inherited from the medieval period toward philosophy, medicine, and science. Printing with **movable type** meant that books no longer needed to be laboriously copied, and this enabled new ideas to spread more rapidly than ever before. This led to a "renaissance," or rebirth, of learning. During this time, the magnetic compass, together with the evolution of new types of sailing ships, enabled a host of European adventurers to explore the world. This led to the discovery of the Americas, and other voyages that spanned the globe.

Shipbuilders developed more efficient ships for transportation, exploration, and warfare.

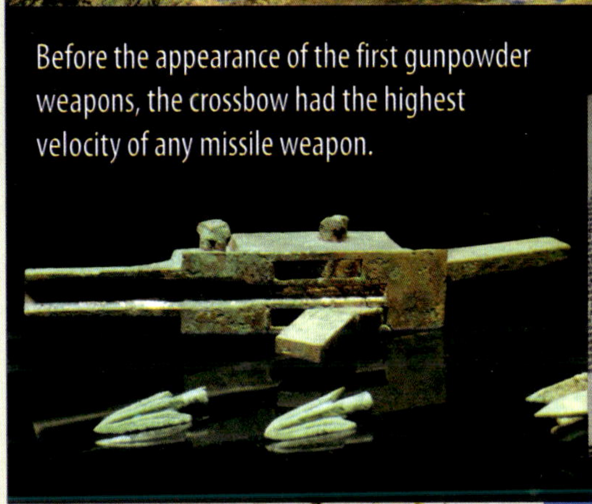

In the early medieval period, some technological achievements of the Romans, such as aqueducts, fell into disrepair.

Before the appearance of the first gunpowder weapons, the crossbow had the highest velocity of any missile weapon.

The invention of printing made it easier to circulate books, and ideas, widely.

Warfare depended on the development of castles to withstand enemy sieges.

Viking explorers used advanced navigation skills to reach North America and build a settlement in the 1000s.

ACTIVITIES

Video

Voyages of Christopher Columbus

Examine the video on the voyages of Columbus.

1. Why did some geographers believe the world was flat, not round, in the 1400s? Why is Columbus' discovery of the Americas often used as a rough approximation to the end of the Middle Ages?
2. Why was Columbus' first voyage paid for by the rulers of Spain? Why was reaching China considered to be such an important goal? Support your answers.

Weblink

History of Technology

Examine the overview of medieval science and technology presented in this weblink.

1. Why were watermills and windmills so important in medieval society? Summarize the uses of mills in medieval Europe.
2. Compare the efficiency of overshot and undershot water wheels. Describe the chemical changes that occur during the making of soap using medieval technology.

Early Chinese books, such as *The Diamond Sutra*, were printed on long scrolls that were uncurled to be read.

Chinese Science

Some technological innovations that appeared in Europe during the Middle Ages were not new. In many cases, the so-called "new" technology had existed for centuries. It might have been developed gradually in Europe itself. Other innovations were brought to Europe by traders or travelers from other parts of the world, such as China.

In about 105 AD, for example, a Chinese court official named Ts'ai Lun made sheets of writing material. He used a mixture of mashed tree bark, hemp, rags, and worn-out fishnets to make paper. The first paper was not made in Europe until the 1000s. The oldest-known printed book is also Chinese. *The Diamond Sutra*, a Buddhist text, was printed in 868 AD. In Europe, printing did not begin until the 1440s.

Chemistry and Physics

Chinese books on **alchemy**, also dating from the ninth century, contain formulas for making mixtures that would burn with a sudden flash. These were precursors of gunpowder, which appeared in Europe in the 1200s. A text from about 83 AD mentions a magnetic ladle balanced so that its handle always turns to point south. It is thought to have been used as a compass. Europeans first used the magnetic compass in the late 1100s. In 132 AD, a Chinese scholar called Chang Heng invented an "earthquake weathercock." This was an early seismograph.

An earth tremor unbalanced an inverted pendulum in the device, which swung toward one of eight radiating channels. The pendulum pushed a slider to eject a ball on the outside of the vessel. The side where the ball emerged showed the direction of the earthquake's epicenter.

Astronomy

The Chinese were far more advanced than Europeans in astronomy and mathematics. Astronomy was vital because the emperor preserved a harmonious relationship with the cosmic order by performing rituals according to a strict calendar. The present Chinese calendar emerged in the fourteenth century BC. An extra month was added every two or three years to reconcile the lunar year with the solar year. As well as marking the equinoxes, solstices, and the seasons, the Chinese calendar predicted events such as lunar eclipses and the positions of the planets. Irregular events were seen as omens. Chinese astronomers kept detailed records of eclipses, novas, comets, and sunspots.

The earliest Chinese mathematical text dates from between 400 and 200 BC. It deals with astronomical calculations, but also contains information about arithmetic and **geometry**, including a statement of Pythagoreas' theorem. Mathematicians also noticed the relationship between the pitch of a sound and the physical processes producing it. This led to Chinese harmonics, which were used to tune stone chimes and bells for rituals.

The Nei Ching

In the early Middle Ages, Europeans had little understanding of the human body. European medicine trailed far behind Chinese medicine, which is said to have begun in 2953 BC. The "Nei Ching," a text that was probably written in the third century BC, records that Chinese doctors tried to maintain the body's balance by administering herbal, animal, and mineral substances. They also recommended massage, physical exercise, and breathing exercises, and adjusted patients' diets. Chinese writers made medical diagrams of the human body (below), and developed an extensive knowledge of natural history. In Europe, a similar systematic approach to medicine began in the 800s AD but only made real advances in knowledge during the Renaissance.

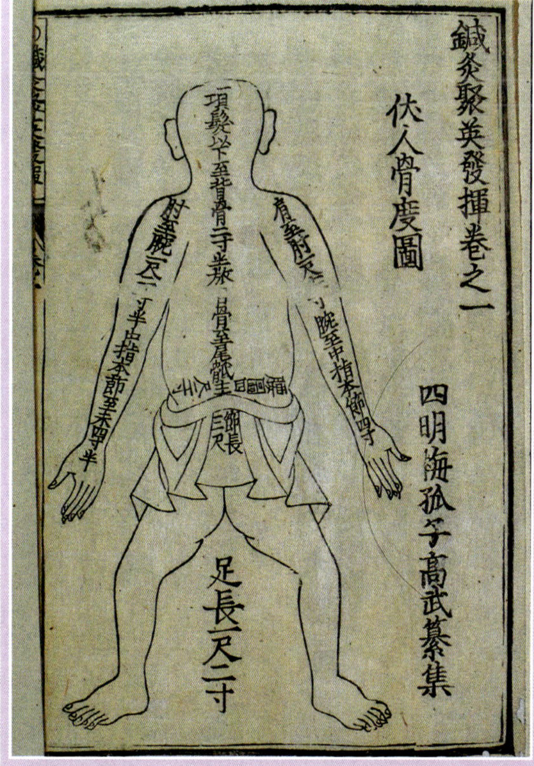

ACTIVITIES

Document

The Nei Ching

Study this document about an early Chinese medical text.

1. Why has the Nei Ching been influential into the twenty-first century? Defend the painful practice of moxibustion.
2. Summarize the core teaching of the Nei Ching. Why does the Nei Ching place such emphasis on using the pulse for diagnosis?

Weblink

Chinese Alchemy

Review the weblink about Chinese alchemy.

1. Why was alchemy discredited in China by the late medieval period, but continued to be important in Europe? Describe how the idea of a constantly changing universe affected Chinese alchemy.
2. Explain why mercury played an important part in Chinese alchemical processes. How might the theories of yin and yang have affected Chinese alchemy and science? Describe the theories.

RUBRIC

Create a Scientific Drawing

Create a scientific drawing of an abacus or counting tray. An exemplary scientific drawing will meet the following criteria:

- Includes a descriptive an accurate title
- The drawing(s) realistically depicts the object(s)
- The drawing only includes features that were actually observed
- Relevant details such as size, colors, textures, shapes, and relationships to surroundings are included
- Multiple perspectives are drawn to provide the viewer with a complete picture
- All parts of the scientific drawing are clearly labeled with the correct terms
- A written explanation of the drawing shows what is included in the drawing
- A key or legend is provided
- An appropriate size and scale is chosen for the drawing so that the details are easily recognized

Counting and the Abacus

During the medieval period, systems of counting developed. Society and the economy grew more complex, so traders needed to keep accurate records of transactions. Officials had to keep records of facts such as land holdings, the numbers of taxpayers, and taxes collected, harvests, food kept in store, and the size of armies.

Recording Numbers

Numerals first came into use in Egypt in about 3400 BC. They consisted of a straight vertical mark for 1, and other symbols for powers of 10, such as 100, 1,000, and so on. Systems of this type worked by grouping. If | means 1, then 2, 3, and 4 are ||, |||, and ||||. The alternative is to use individual symbols for numbers up to a given value. The Chinese devised a system like this in the fourth century BC. It had symbols from 1 to 9, and for 10, 100, and 1,000.

Many cultures count to a base of 10. The Maya counted to base 20, however, and some people counted to base 12, which is why there are 12 inches in 1 foot. The Babylonians counted to base 60. That is why there are 60 seconds in a minute and 60 minutes in an hour, or a degree of arc.

Numeral Systems

At the start of the medieval period, Europeans still used Roman numerals. This used letters as symbols. The Hindu-Arabic numerals in use today first appeared in Europe in 976 AD.

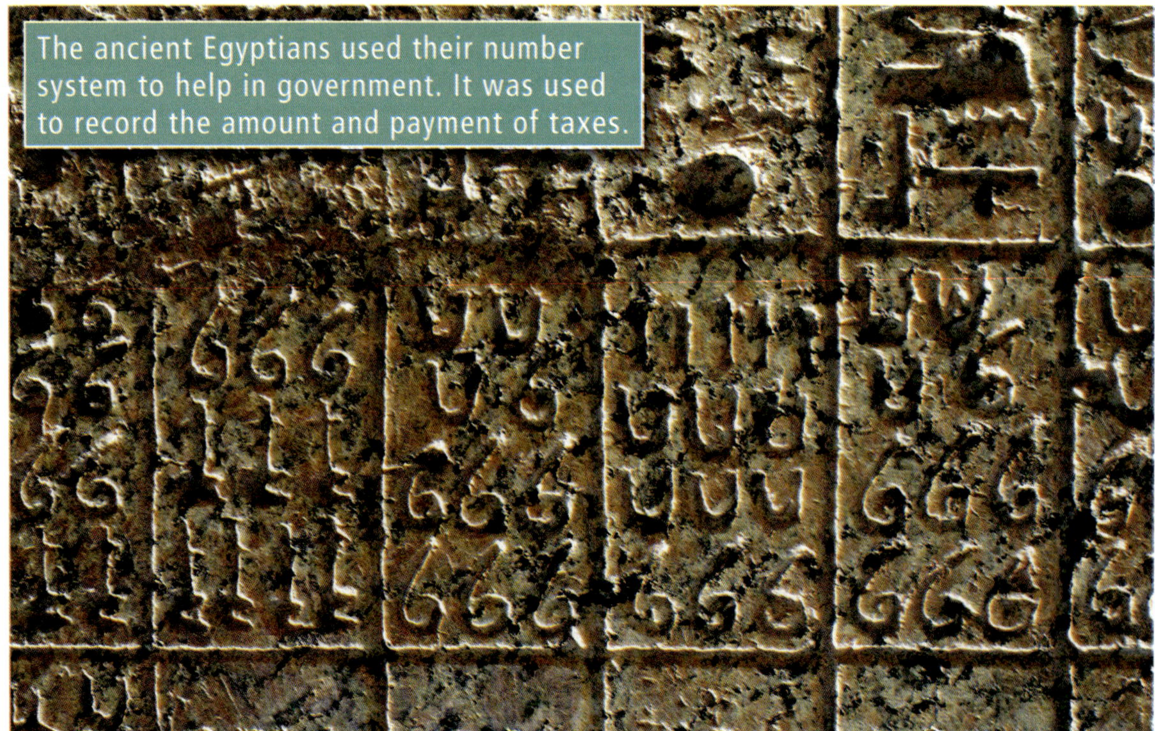

The ancient Egyptians used their number system to help in government. It was used to record the amount and payment of taxes.

Some merchants in China still use an abacus to figure out deals.

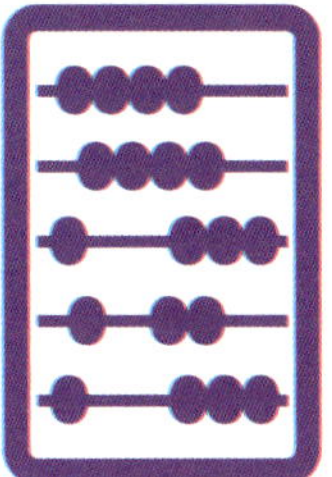

BASE 60

ABACUS

Base 60 is the lowest base number where the fractions of halves, thirds, quarters, fifths, sixths, tenths and twelfths are all whole numbers.

300 BC

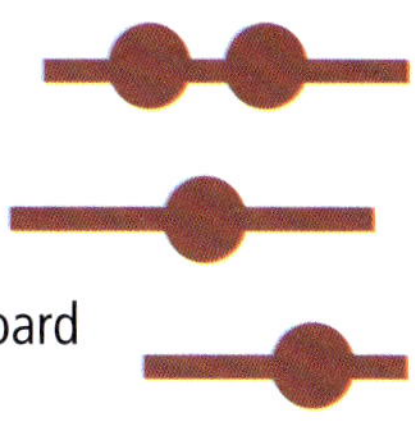

COUNTING BOARDS

The oldest European counting board found so far dates to 300 BC.

The numerals originated in India, probably as early as the fourth century BC. They were in use in 662 AD in Mesopotamia. Arab scholars began using them in the eighth century AD, and Muslim scholars introduced them to Spain in the following century.

The new place-value system was useful for trade. It provides an efficient way of recording quantities and dates, and for performing addition and subtraction. Multiplication and division are more difficult, as is using long numbers, but these were less common. Calculation is easier because the position of a number symbol indicates its value. Numbers are written with the lowest value on the right and the highest on the left. Therefore, 369 means (3 x 100) + (6 x 10) + 9 because of the position of each numeral. Several documents suggest that the place-value system originated early, but it is uncertain when. The first clear record of a place-value system with a symbol for zero dates from 876. It came from Gwalior in Delhi, India.

Counting Boards

Despite not having a place-value system for writing numbers, early mathematicians performed complex calculations using a counting board. This device was probably invented in Babylon as a board on which sand was spread to provide a writing medium. The Semitic word for dust is abq, and the Greeks called a counting board an abax. Today, it is known as an abacus.

The Chinese had also invented the counting board by the fourth century BC. A Chinese book written in 190 AD clearly describes a primitive abacus. An abacus that used beads on wires was in use in China by 1500 AD. The Chinese abacus reached Japan in about 1600 AD.

ACTIVITIES

Video

A Big Zero: The Bakhshali Manuscript

Review this University of Oxford video about a surprisingly early discovery of the use of zero.

1. Why is the age of zero so surprising to modern scholars? Explain the difficulties of math without zero.
2. Why is the Indian zero so revolutionary? Explain the difference between a placeholder and zero.

Weblink

The Abacus: A Brief History

Examine the description of early counting technology.

1. Why might a base ten system be a good counting system? Explain the disadvantages of a base ten system.
2. Why might sand have been an important feature of early counting boards? Summarize the advantage of the abacus in math teaching.

The longest of Rome's 11 stone aqueducts carried water 60 miles (97 kilometers) into the city.

Aqueducts and Dams

Water and its management was vital in the medieval period. Rivers provided means of transportation for people and goods. Water powered machines, and it was also vital for agriculture to grow crops to support the expanding population.

People in the Middle Ages used various mechanical devices for lifting water for agriculture. Some had been invented in the ancient world, and some are still in use in parts of the world today. They include the shadoof. The shadoof is a balanced pole with a **counterweight** for raising water out of ditches. The saqiya is a chain of pots worked by animal power. The pots are dipped into water and then lifted on the chain and emptied at a higher level The Archimedes' screw is a screw-shaped device turned by hand to lift water. The noria is a water-driven wheel that lifts water automatically. Ancient peoples also used forms of pump.

Water Supply

Large-scale water-supply systems began in the ancient world. The best-known is that of the Roman Empire. In order to supply fountains and bathhouses, the Romans built long aqueducts from springs in the hills. For crossing deep valleys, they sometimes used inverted siphons. These pipes conveyed water down a gradient and up the other side. Siphons work if the pipes are kept full of water and release the water at a lower level than it originally entered.

Building an Aqueduct

Roman surveyors planned routes to ensure aqueducts would flow downhill so water would not stagnate. They tapped springs in hilly regions to ensure a sufficient fall in elevation over the necessary distance. Generally, water ran in a conduit close to the surface, following the contours of the land. If it met a ridge, then tunneling was required. If it hit a valley, a bridge was built to maintain the gradient. Sometimes, a pressurized pipe system was installed. This was known as an inverted siphon. It used pressure generated by the water's rush down one side of the valley to push it up the other side. Along its path, the conduit had manhole shafts in order to allow maintenance. When the aqueduct reached the city's outskirts, water ran into a large distribution tank called the main castellum. From there, smaller conduits carried it to the various districts of the city.

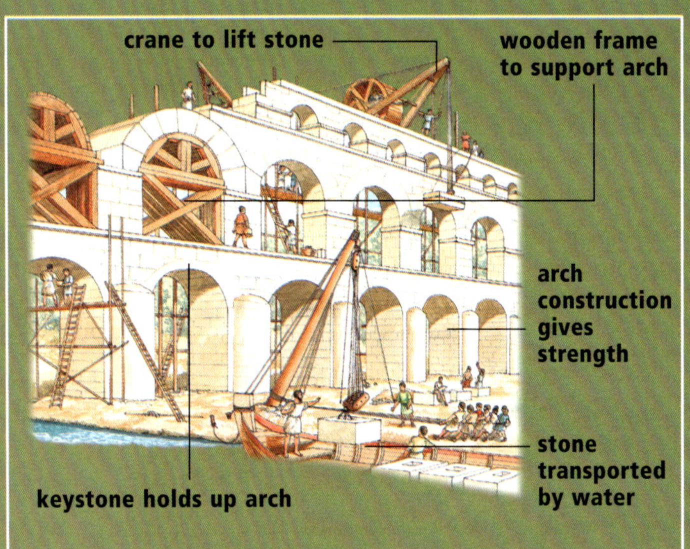

After the fall of the Roman Empire in 476, people returned to getting their water from rivers or from wells. This water was sometimes dirty and carried diseases.

Rivers and Flood Control

Many civilizations have grown up around large rivers, yet most rivers flood. On China's Huang He or Yellow River, for example, flood-control began thousands of years ago. It continued in the medieval period. Ways to protect against flooding included deepening and straightening the river channel. People also built high banks called levees, and dug overflow channels. Rivers are complex systems, however, so raising banks to prevent floods in one place sometimes made flooding worse elsewhere.

Dams

Dams have been used since early times, mainly to store water or divert it for irrigation. Most early developments in dam design came in the Middle East. The region lacks regular rainfall, so as civilizations emerged and grew, peoples such as the Babylonians wanted to be able to trap water when the rivers were full.

ACTIVITIES

Transparency

Building an Aqueduct

Review the diagram showing how Roman aqueducts were constructed.

1. Explain the importance of the inverted siphon in aqueduct construction. Why did the pipes in the siphon need to be full of water to make it work?
2. Describe methods by which the Romans might have been able to calculate small differences in height above sea level over several miles (km) in order to keep water flowing downhill. Describe the type of maintenance that Roman engineers would have carried out on aqueducts.

Weblink

Aqueducts: Quenching Rome's Thirst

Examine the weblink about these massive Roman engineering projects.

1. How were Roman water tunnels made waterproof? How dangerous was the digging of tunnels for watercourses?
2. Why were Roman aqueducts often neglected during the medieval period? Why are aqueducts a healthy way of delivering water to a city?

RUBRIC

Write an Abstract

Use your library or Google Scholar to find a scientific research article or study comparing the use of watermills in medieval Europe and China. Write a 300-word abstract. An exemplary abstract will meet the following criteria.

- Introductory statement is clear, concise, and engaging, and connects the topic to other research
- Purpose is clear, concise, and relevant
- Explains what methods the scientific historians used to answer their research question
- Explanation of the findings includes what was expected, discovered, accomplished, collected, and produced
- Clearly states how the article or study advances knowledge about the topic, why it is important, and how it can be used
- Writing is appropriate and is free from grammatical errors

Water Power

Water power was important during the medieval period. Using water to drive a wheel made milling grain much easier. A waterwheel is a wheel fitted with a set of vanes or paddles that cause the wheel to turn when water flows past them. A shaft connected to the center of the wheel rotates and drives some sort of mechanism, such as a pair of millstones for grinding grain.

Horizontal Waterwheels

The simplest type of waterwheel is a horizontal waterwheel, sometimes called a Greek or Norse mill. This wheel has a vertical shaft that can be connected directly to a millstone. The wheel is mounted in a fast-flowing stream, or water from a channel is directed onto the vanes of the wheel. In the past, horizontal wheels were mounted within the arches of river bridges, or even on barges moored in midstream.

Vertical Waterwheels

Other waterwheels can be mounted vertically and drive a horizontal shaft. There are various types. In an undershot wheel, the lower paddles dip into a stream. As with other vertical wheels, there has to be some sort of gear arrangement to make the horizontal shaft turn the millstones.

An undershot waterwheel is driven by water channeled from a river into a narrow mill race, to provide a constant water flow.

Because of their weight, millstones are nearly always mounted horizontally. The undershot wheel depends on a more or less constant rate of water flow. To ensure such a flow, engineers often dammed the main stream, creating a reservoir that guaranteed a constant current of water, known as a millrace. The undershot wheel is sometimes called a Vitruvian wheel for the first-century-BC Roman architect, Marcus Vitruvius Pollio, who described it in detail in about 20 BC.

With an overshot waterwheel, the water arrives at the top of the wheel, usually along a channel or trough called a launder. The paddles are angled or curved to create small "buckets." The weight of falling water held in the buckets makes the wheel turn. It is also possible to angle the paddles the opposite way, so that the wheel rotates in the same direction as the flow. This is called a pitchback wheel. The overshot wheel is more efficient than the undershot wheel. It generates about 3 **horsepower** from a 6-foot (2-m) wheel, compared to only 0.5 horsepower from a similar undershot wheel. In about 300 AD, the Romans built a flour mill at Barbegal in southern France with 16 overshot wheels that generated more than 30 horsepower.

The overshot waterwheel requires less water than an undershot wheel, so it does not always have to be built next to a fast-flowing stream. It costs more to build than an undershot wheel, but is more efficient on all other counts. It was the favored waterwheel for more than 1,000 years. At the end of the eleventh century, there were nearly 6,000 watermills in England alone.

Giant wooden norias are still used in Middle Eastern countries such as Syria to raise water for irrigation.

As well as powering flour mills, waterwheels were used to drive saws for cutting stone and slicing logs, and for lifting water for irrigation. In China, they were used to power mechanical water clocks. Waterwheels called norias, up to 40 feet (12 m) across, were positioned on rivers in Middle Eastern countries. They supplied water to neighboring fields.

ACTIVITIES

Weblink

Waterwheels and Gear Arrangements

Examine the descriptions of early waterwheel and gear arrangements.

1. Explain the importance of gears in an undershot mill wheel. Why is an overshot wheel more difficult to create than an undershot wheel?
2. Why were there so few Roman undershot mill wheels? Explain how a trip hammer connected to a Chinese watermill would work.

Arabian Science

The prophet Mohammad founded Islam in Arabia in about 630 AD. Over the next century, his teachings spread throughout an empire that extended from central Asia to Spain. The rise of Islam was accompanied by a rise in learning as scholars studied ancient texts.

In 750, the capital of the Islamic empire moved to Baghdad under the Abbasid caliphs. In about 820, the seventh caliph, Abdallah al-Ma'mun, ordered the creation of an observatory for astronomers and a library as part of an academy called Bayt al-Hikma, The House of Wisdom.

Al-Ma'mun's astronomers accurately calculated the inclination of the plane of the ecliptic, which is the angle between Earth's rotational axis and its orbital plane. They also calculated the circumference of Earth as 20,400 miles (32,824 km). The correct figure is 24,875 miles (40,030 km).

The Arabian alchemist Abu Musa Jabir Ibn-Hayyan is often known as Geber. He expanded a Greek idea that all matter is made from four elements, which are earth, air, fire, and water. Geber believed the elements combine to form two substances, sulfur and mercury. These two substances could be combined to make any metal, including gold, with the help of a substance called al-iksir, or "elixir."

The Abbasid caliphs invited scholars from all over the Middle East and Europe to study at the House of Wisdom.

Medical Discoveries

In about 900, Abu-Bakr Muhammad ibn-Zakariya al-Rhazi, or Rhazes, became chief physician at the main hospital in Baghdad. He is said to have been the first person to make a clear distinction between measles and smallpox. He was also an alchemist. Like Geber, he was meticulous in his experiments. He left such detailed notes that later scientists have been able to replicate his work. Rhazes prepared plaster of Paris and described its use for making casts to hold broken limbs in place.

The ideas of Ptolemy, the ancient Greek scientist, continued to influence medieval astronomers and geographers.

Arabic Numerals

The modern system of numerals is based on the work of the Arabian mathematician Abu Jafar Muhammad ibn-Musa al-Khwarizmi. Al-Khwarizmi studied Hindu and Greek sources and used Hindu numerals, including zero, in his own works, which were later translated from Arabic into Latin. He lived in Baghdad, where he had the important post of chief librarian at the House of Wisdom.

In about 830, Al-Khwarizmi wrote *Hisab al-jabr w'al-muqabala*, "Calculation by Restoration and Reduction." This treatise on mathematics became highly influential. In Latin, *al-jabr*, "restoration," became "algebra."

Astronomy

Arabian **astronomers** preserved the ideas of the second-century-AD Greek astronomer Ptolemy. Most astronomers accepted Ptolemy's work, but in about 880, Abu-Abdullah Muhammad ibn-Jabir al-Battani, also called Albategnius, observed that when the Sun appeared at its smallest, its position in the sky was not where Ptolemy said it was. Albategnius deduced that this position, called aphelion, when the Sun is farthest from Earth, changes slowly. He figured out fairly accurately the rate of its motion. This allowed him to measure the length of the year more accurately. Calendar makers were still using his measurement centuries later.

ACTIVITIES

Document

The Writings of Rhazes on Kidney Diseases

Review this description of the writings of a noted Islamic scholar.

1. Why was kidney disease such an important problem in the medieval middle east? Why was black urine a significant symptom?
2. Summarize Rhazes' advice for avoiding kidney and bladder stones. Describe why forceps were an improvement on the previous technology used to extract stones.

Weblink

Arabian Astronomy in the Middle Ages

Assess the weblink on Arabian astronomy.

1. Why did the Bedouin divide the sky into 28 segments? Describe how pre-Islamic Arabian traditions linked with ancient Greek astronomical observations in the Middle Ages.
2. Explain the importance of the "Book of the Constellations of the Fixed Stars" by Abd al-Rahman ibn Umar al-Sufi. Describe how concepts of Islamic astronomy reached European scholars during the sixteenth century.

RUBRIC

Analyzing Bias in a Document

Students will analyze the bias that exists in a document from a different scientific time and place, and how that bias shapes the opinions presented in the document. An exemplary analysis of bias in a document will meet the following criteria.

- Identifies the main points presented in the document
- Offers an in-depth interpretation of the document
- Differentiates between facts and opinions
- Identifies and presents information about the writer
- Assesses the writer's reliability
- Determines the goals of the document
- Considers and assesses the writer's perspective
- Determines the writer's intended audience
- Describes the scientific context for the time and place in which the document was created, and analyze how this context might have shaped the opinions expressed in the document
- Infers what political or societal influences might have shaped the opinions presented in the document
- Determines whether the writer had first-hand knowledge on the topic or event, or whether he or she is reporting as a secondary source
- Determines the bias in the document
- Explores other sources related to the topic of the document to compare perspectives and facts

The Egyptians crushed papyrus stalks to separate the fibers, which they dried to form thin sheets for writing.

Making and Using Paper

There was no paper in the ancient world. From about 2800 BC, the Egyptians made papyrus using reeds that grew along the Nile River. Papyrus is the root of the word *paper*. Other writing surfaces were parchment, made from sheepskins, and vellum. That was a thinner material made from lamb or calf skin.

The first reference to paper comes in about 105 AD, from the Chinese writer Ts'ai Lun. He describes making paper from rags and other materials, such as tree bark. One method involved taking bamboo fibers and the inner bark of a mulberry tree. The fibers and bark were pounded together in water. The resulting slurry was poured through a piece of cloth stretched on a frame. The water trickled through, while the fibers left on the cloth dried to form paper.

Despite Chinese attempts to keep it secret, knowledge of papermaking spread to Korea, Japan, and Vietnam. Travelers introduced the process to India and to Samarkand in central Asia, and by the eighth century, it had reached Damascus and Baghdad.

The first European papermaking plant was built in 1150 near Valencia, Spain. By then, paper factories were called mills. This was because the process of breaking up fibers for paper used similar waterwheels and grindstones as those used to mill grain into flour.

Making Paper

Paper was originally made one sheet at a time. People dipped a wire-mesh frame into a vat of stock made from woodpulp or rags beaten to separate the fibers. When the frame was lifted out, water was allowed to drain from the thin layer of pulp. The sheet was then left to dry.

The First Books

The forerunners of books were scrolls. These were long strips of papyrus, bamboo, or **silk** rolled around a stick. During the Middle Ages, however, codexes came to replace scrolls. These were sheets of parchment gathered into bundles, folded in half, stitched together, and protected by wood or leather covers. Pages made it easier for readers to follow and find their place.

The Coming of Printing

Texts and pictures printed from carved woodblocks first appeared in China in about 600 AD. They were produced by pressing the paper against the inked woodblock with a flat piece of wood. Reusable pieces of type made from clay, and later tin, were developed in China in about 1040. They never caught on because there were too many characters in Chinese for this method to be practical. European printers had the advantage of a 26-letter alphabet, which was much better adapted to movable type. In 1438, a German goldsmith named Johannes Gutenberg developed his own technique of typecasting. He opened the first **printing press** in Mainz, Germany, in about 1450.

Chinese Paper Money

The Venetian merchant Marco Polo traveled to China in the late 1200s. On his return, he wrote a famous account of his time in East Asia. Polo described many things that were unknown in Europe, including the use of paper for many purposes. He reported that the Chinese used paper money, which was an important part of their economy. He described how the money was made from the bark of the mulberry tree. He also said that the paper money had intrinsic value because the emperor was prepared to back up its face value. Foreign merchants, however, may not have been as eager as Polo suggests to accept paper money in return for their pearls and precious stones.

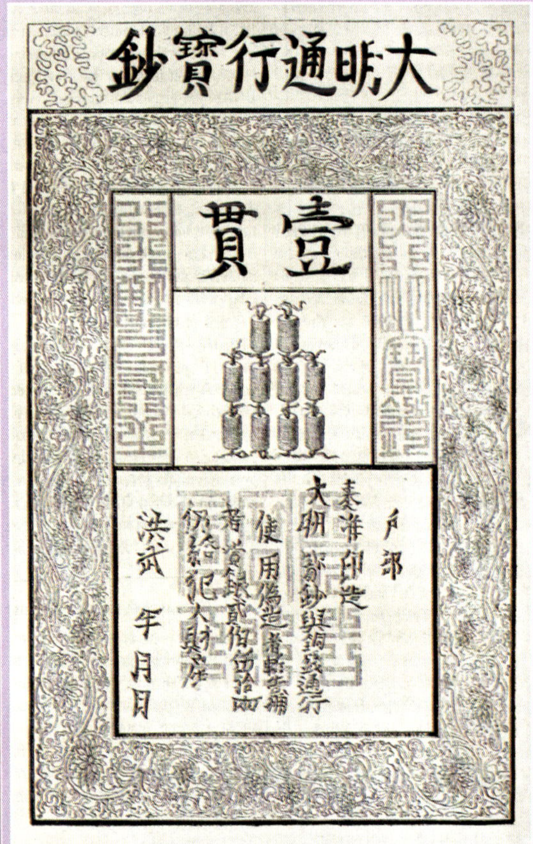

ACTIVITIES

First Hand

Marco Polo's account of his trip to East Asia Describing Chinese paper Money

Read Marco Polo's account of his trip to East Asia.

1. Does the description of how Kublai Khan created money seem accurate? What are the drawbacks of simply printing money as a form of exchange?
2. Would it be simple to forge the paper money Marco Polo describes? Why might people not do so? Justify any conclusions.

Weblink

Paper in Ancient China

Analyze the weblink on papermaking in Ancient China.

1. Why did the use of paper and printing distinguish China from other ancient cultures of the time? What were the differences?
2. Explain how the "secrets" of Chinese paper and papermaking eventually reached the outside world. What was the importance of the spread of such knowledge? Describe the effect it had on the exchange of ideas worldwide.

RUBRIC

Analyzing a Primary Source

Students will complete a thorough analysis of a primary source. An exemplary analysis will meet the following criteria.

- Identifies the creator of the source
- Explains what medium was used to create the primary source
- Describes why the source qualifies as a primary one
- Explores any literary devices used in the source
- Identifies the intended audience for the source
- Relates the creators goals in creating the source
- Illustrates knowledge of the period and location in which the source was created
- Distinguishes between facts and opinions found in the source
- Examines the reliability of the sources creator
- Compares the source with similar documents
- Cites additional sources used in the analysis
- Presents information in a clear, concise manner
- Uses correct spelling, grammar, and punctuation

Viking Voyages

The Vikings, or Norsemen, were intrepid sailors. They made voyages that were longer than any known before. As early as 793 AD, Norsemen plundered islands off Scotland and Holland. While some Vikings invaded Britain and France, others began a series of voyages across the northern Atlantic Ocean.

In 982, Erik Thorvaldson, or Erik the Red, discovered Greenland, adopting the attractive name to encourage settlers. In about 1000, his son Leif Eriksson explored the coast of North America. He found a place he called Vinland, translated as "Wineland," probably for the grapes he found there. Later, Eriksson took settlers to Newfoundland, where they briefly settled at L'Anse aux Meadows. The Vikings also raided much of Europe by sailing up major rivers. They attacked Paris, France, in 845 and 856. They set up settlements, such as Normandy in northern France.

Longships

The secret of the Vikings' success at sea was an open-decked vessel. This was called a longship. Sleek and fast, it had a double-ended hull and a mast carrying a large square sail.

The Vikings settled the inhospitable territory of Greenland from the late 900s until the early 1400s.

A bank of oars along each side was used for maneuvering near shore. The oars could also give the vessel more speed in battle. There was a single steering oar on the righthand side. The Vikings called the largest type of longship a *drekar*, or dragon ship, for the snarling dragons' heads carved at each end. Up to 100 feet (30 m) long, it could sail at up to 14 knots, the equivalent of 16 miles per hour (26 kilometers per hour).

Life on Board

The boatbuilders used overlapping oak planks to make the sides of the hull, fixed in place with iron nails. They made the inner structure of the hull from timber selected from curved branches. The sail was a sheet of woven wool. It became difficult to handle when it was soaking wet in a storm. The sailors slept on the open deck in sleeping bags made from animal skins, and ate dried or salted meat or fish. They carried fresh water, but they also drank mead, a drink made from fermented honey.

Boat Burials

Much knowledge of Viking longships comes from ship burials. In 1904, a ship burial was excavated at Oseberg in Norway. Queen Asa had been buried in 834. The ship was dragged onto the shore and lowered into a shallow pit. It was covered with stones and clay, with a layer of turf on top. It lay undisturbed for more than 1,000 years before it was rediscovered in a remarkably well preserved condition.

Ohthere and Wulfstan

Ohthere and Wulfstan were Viking sailors who both left accounts of sailing east from Norway. Ohthere sailed north, around the northern edge of Norway and into the White Sea. He later headed down toward what is now northern Russia. Ohthere describes hunting for whales and killing walruses for their ivory, and says that the local people herded reindeer. The "Finnas," who lived in the interior parts of Scandinavia, paid tribute to the Vikings in the form of furs and ropes made of sealskin.

Wulfstan also voyaged east from Norway, but his route took him north through the Baltic Sea, with Sweden on his west. Wulfstan went east of the mouth of the Vistula, a river he identified as marking an important frontier. He then described the funeral rites of chieftains among the people he met living east of the Vistula.

ACTIVITIES

Document

Ohthere and Wulfstan's Accounts of Their Voyages

Read the accounts of these early Viking voyages.

1. What species of whale would the Vikings have hunted? Why are reindeer so suitable as the basis of a pastoral society? Explain your theories.
2. Do the accounts imply that oars or sails were equally important for the propulsion of Viking longships? Why would animal skins have been so valuable to the Vikings?

Video

The Viking Longship

Analyze the video of Viking longships.

1. Why were Viking ships generally more maneuverable and seaworthy than previous European vessels? How did the Vikings make their ships watertight?
2. Why was it better to make planks using axes and adzes rather than saws? Describe the advantages of clinker-built construction.

Wind Power

The first windmills appeared in about 605 in Persia, present-day Iran. They pumped water into irrigation systems and ground grain to make flour. Windmills arrived in western Europe in the 1100s. They differed from Persian devices in one important respect. Instead of being mounted on a vertical axis, their sails radiated out from a horizontal axis, supported on the side of a post or a stone tower. Europeans devised gears to move the turning force through 90 degrees to drive the millstone. The technology had been invented for use with waterwheels.

These mills had to face the wind for the sails to turn efficiently. The first European windmills were built facing the prevailing wind or were adjustable. The former solution worked well on Mediterranean coasts, where the wind nearly always blew in off the sea. Farther north, the winds were more variable. The solution was to build post mills, which were small and mounted on a single stout post that could be turned to face the wind.

Rotating Windmills

By the fifteenth century, windmill sails were mounted in a free-rotating cap sitting on the main tower. When the miller needed to adjust the direction the sails were facing, he only had to turn the cap, not the whole structure. This was usually done using a long pole attached to the back of the cap. Pushing the pole turned the whole cap. This advance meant that the size of windmills was no longer restricted by the need to turn them around. Mill towers could be built of brick or stone, several stories high.

The flat plains of central Spain were home to about 32 windmills built from the 1000s onward.

Structure of a Windmill

This windmill was designed to mill grain to produce flour, but other windmills have been designed to pump water out of fields or generate electricity. The mill has four large, wooden sails arranged in a cross. Attached to the center of this cross inside the windmill is the windshaft. This is a sturdy wooden axle that supports the sails and turns with them. The sails are of a type known as spring sails. They have small wooden shutters that blow open when the wind is strong, preventing the sails from spinning around too quickly. Earlier sails were covered in cloth that the miller had to roll up to slow down the sails. As the sails rotate, the windshaft turns the brake wheel, which in turn rotates a series of gears, starting with the wallower. The wallower turns the great spur wheel, which turns the gears that move the millstones. The millstones are large, circular stones that crush the grain between them. Some windmills have a central post that allows the whole mill to rotate, so no matter what direction the wind is blowing, the mill still works.

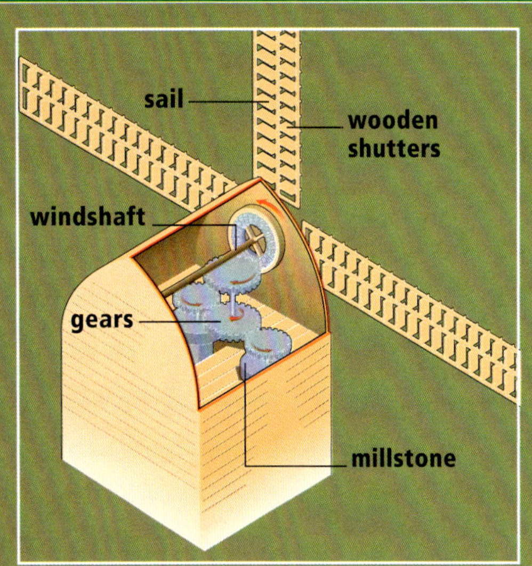

Windmills had become proper buildings, not just machines. Building them higher meant larger sails that generated more power. The first sails were canvas mounted on wooden frames. The sails could be furled in strong winds, or taken off when not in use. In 1772, the Scottish millwright Andrew Meikle invented spring sails. These were made from wooden slats held shut by springs.

Uses For Windmills

Early windmills were used to pump water and grind grain. These roles were important in Holland. There, large areas of low-lying farmland were kept dry only by the constant activity of thousands of windmills. The mills pumped out water from the fields into canals.

European settlers introduced the windmill to the New World in the 16th century. The Halladay mill, patented by U.S. machinist Daniel Halladay in 1854, played a major role in the settlement of the West. It had a tail fin that turned it to follow the direction of the wind. Thousands of similar windmills are still used to pump groundwater to the surface for livestock all over the rural United States and the Outback in Australia.

ACTIVITIES

Document

Daniel Halladay and the Halladay Mill

Review the patent application for the Halladay windmill.

1. Describe the use of water in the working of the windmill. Why is a ball governor required for grinding, churning, and threshing?
2. Which mechanical arrangement was Halladay looking to patent? Which mechanical arrangement was he not seeking to patent?

Transparency

Structure of a Windmill

Examine the diagram of a European windmill.

1. Why were spring sails such an important invention? Describe how the spring sail mechanism may have worked?
2. Summarize the advantages and disadvantages of windmills mounted on a central post. Explain whether the height of a windmill would make any difference to the gearing mechanism.

RUBRIC

Analyzing a Scientific Video

Students will watch and assess a video related to a scientific discovery, and write an analysis of the video. An exemplary video analysis will meet the following criteria.

- Identifies the purpose of the video
- Identifies the intended audience of the video
- Identifies the video as a primary or secondary source
- Discusses the scientific and social context of the video
- Describes how the content of the video is presented
- Summarizes the information and opinions presented in the video
- Analyzes the quality of the content presented in the video
- Assesses the effectiveness of the video
- Determines whether the images and graphics used in the video relate to the content
- Determines whether the video is easy to follow and understand
- Gives the analysis a clear and consistent purpose
- Organizes the analysis in a logical, effective manner
- Presents a strong, clear argument about the video
- Provides strong and accurate details to support the argument about the video
- Considers other perspectives on the purpose and effectiveness of the video
- Cites all sources used in the analysis

Luca Pacioli invented a form of accounting in which every deal is recorded twice, as a credit and a debit.

Advances in Math

European scholars traveled widely in the Middle Ages, and some even learned Arabic. The English philosopher Adelard of Bath was one of the most prolific translators of works from Arabic into Latin. Arabic numerals made a big difference to the way that European scholars thought about math.

The Italian mathematician Leonardo Fibonacci explained how to use Arabic numerals in *Liber Abaci*, or "Book of Calculation," in 1202. Fibonacci outlined the advantages of a number system using place values. He also used a bar to form fractions, such as 1/4. Fibonacci wrote about number series. In the series that bears his name, each number is the sum of the two preceding numbers. It begins 1, 1, 2, 3, 5, 8, 13, 21, and so on.

Another major breakthrough came in 1494. The Italian monk Luca Pacioli invented **double-entry bookkeeping**. He described the process in *Summa de Arithmetica, Geometrica, Proportioni, et Proportionalita*, "Everything about Arithmetic, Geometry, and Proportion." He is seen as the founder of accountancy.

Early mathematical works were all written for scholars or merchants. The first popular English book on mathematics was *The Ground of Artes*.

It was published in English in 1543 by the English scholar Robert Recorde. The book remained in print for more than 150 years. In 1557, Recorde became the first European to use the equal sign, or =. The plus and minus signs, + and –, were introduced in Europe by German mathematicians.

Algebra

Originally, mathematicians wrote out algebraic equations in words. The unknown was called *cosa* in Latin and *Coss* in German. Then, in 1591, the French lawyer and statesman François Viète wrote *In Artem Analytica Isogoge*, "Introduction to the Analytic Art." Viète used vowels to stand for unknown quantities, and consonants for known ones. He produced the first algebraic equations that a modern mathematician would recognize. Viète is sometimes called the "father of algebra."

Decimals

Simon Stevin, also known as Stevinus, was a Flemish physicist, engineer, and mathematician. He partially introduced decimal notation into mathematics in 1585. Decimal fractions could not be used fully until John Napier's adoption of the decimal point over 30 years later.

In about 1622, the English mathematician William Oughtred invented the **slide rule**. Engineers and mathematicians used slide rules until the introduction of the electronic calculator in the late 1900s. Oughtred marked two rulers with logarithmic scales. Calculations were made mechanically by moving one ruler against the other and reading off the solution. In a book published in 1631, Oughtred also introduced the symbols * for multiplication and :: for proportionality.

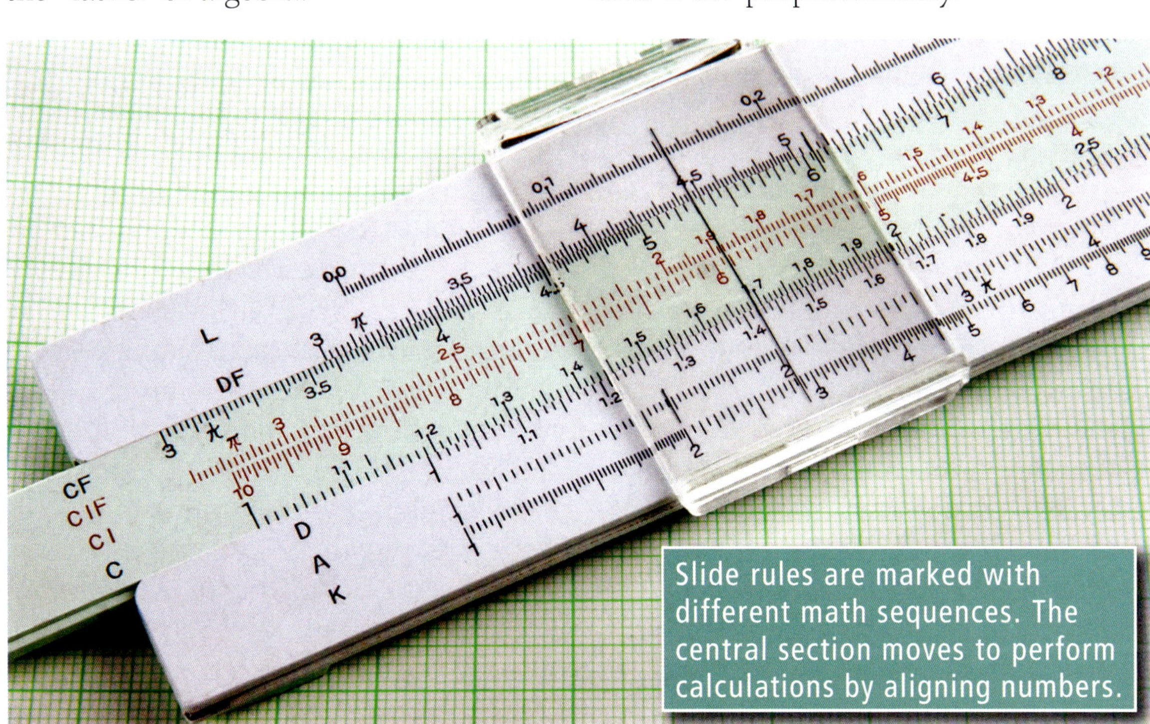

Slide rules are marked with different math sequences. The central section moves to perform calculations by aligning numbers.

ACTIVITIES

First Hand

Luca Pacioli and Double-entry Bookkeeping

Read the translated pages of Luca Pacioli's book.

1. Why was Pacioli described as the founder of accountancy? What basic similarities could be drawn between the processes described by Pacioli and double-entry bookkeeping today?
2. Why did Pacioli feel the need to write such a book? Who was it aimed at? Would merchants and scholars have used it? Assess the impact such a work would have had on the merchant society in 1494.

Weblink

How a Slide Rule Works

Review the video on the slide rule.

1. Summarize the main mathematical applications of the slide rule. Why does the slide rule give an approximation rather than a precise answer to many problems?
2. Describe the advantages of the circular slide rule. How does the logarithmic scale apply to slide rules?

Placing a castle on a motte ensured that any attackers had to approach uphill, giving the defenders above an advantage.

Castles

A castle is a fortified building. Originally constructed as strongholds for kings or lords, castles were designed to command a wide view of the countryside. They were built to be as impregnable as their builders could make them.

After William of Normandy invaded England in 1066, he built a series of castles in a style found throughout Europe. The stronghold, or keep, was usually built of wood. It stood on top of a mound, or motte, surrounded by a ditch. At the foot of the motte were areas, called wards, protected by wooden palisades. These were fences made of stakes. A ward protected by walls is called a bailey, so these were named motte-and-bailey castles.

Defending The Castle

As time went on, important castles were increasingly built from stone. The center of every castle was the keep, or *donjon*. This was the most heavily fortified part of the castle. It was the place to which the defenders would retreat if an enemy broke through the outer walls. The keep contained the owner's living quarters, offices, and stores. It had a well, and was equipped to withstand a long siege. In later castles, it became customary to build the residential quarters in the bailey, leaving the keep as the last line of defense.

Increasingly the outer wall of the castle was protected by one or more moats. There were sometimes baileys between the moats. Château Gaillard, on a cliff above the Seine River in France, for example, has three baileys.

There is an inner bailey between the foot of the motte and the inner moat, a middle bailey between the inner moat and the outer walls, and an outer bailey outside the walls, protected by an outer moat. An invader would have to overcome all three baileys to reach the keep. King Richard I of England built the castle between 1196 and 1198. It was one of the strongest castles in Europe.

For 200 years after 1095, European knights called Crusaders set out on a series of invasions of the Holy Land. They built many castles to protect the territory they captured from the local Muslim rulers. One of the most imposing was the Krak des Chevaliers in Syria. The castle dominated a strategic pass. With an inner and outer wall separated by a wide ditch, it could accommodate a total of 2,000 soldiers. The Knights of St. John, also known as the Knights Hospitallers, built the castle. They held it from 1142 until the Egyptian sultan Baybars I captured it in 1271.

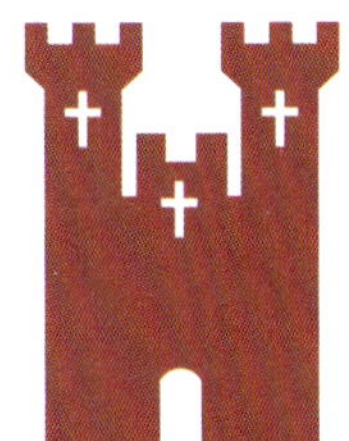

36

NORMAN CASTLES

Between 1066 and 1087, William the Conqueror built 36 castles to secure his hold on England.

4,000

SWISS CASTLES

There were 4,000 castles in medieval Switzerland.

Luxurious Palaces

Castles became obsolete when gunpowder weapons emerged. Cannonballs were able to break down stone castle walls. In 1494, French troops advanced through Italy using artillery to destroy every castle in their way. Kings and lords gave up building castles. Instead, they began to build themselves palaces. These new structures were built for display and comfort, rather than for defense during warfare.

The Krak des Chevaliers was not defeated in war. The defenders were tricked into surrender.

ACTIVITIES

Video

Krak des Chevaliers Video

Review this video of the well-preserved crusader castle.

1. Describe why the guard towers of the castle are rounded rather than square. What were the most important storage areas of the castle?
2. From the images in the video, how do you think the defenders could deal with attackers who reached the foot of the outer walls? Were there any weaknesses in Krak des Chevaliers?

Weblink

Motte-and-bailey (Norman) Castles in Europe

Examine the weblink on motte and bailey castles.

1. How important were existing local features such as mounds or rivers to the creation of motte and bailey castles? Why were so many motte and bailey castles built in England after the Norman conquest?
2. Explain the importance of the motte. What were the main weaknesses of motte and bailey castles?

RUBRIC

Analyzing a Scientific Biography

Students will research the life of Copernicus and present their findings. An exemplary biographical analysis will meet the following criteria.

- Illustrates strong knowledge of the subject
- Identifies the author of the biography
- Describes why the subject of the biography is important
- Contains information about the time and place in which the subject was born
- Lists important events in the subject's life
- Explains how events in the subject's life impacted him or her
- Makes inferences about the subject based on events in his or her life
- Explains how the subject influenced the world while he or she lived
- Researches the cultural and historical context of the subject's life
- Examines the effect that the subject has had on the modern world
- Supplements information from the biography with independent research
- Organizes the analysis in a logical, effective manner
- Uses correct spelling, grammar, and punctuation
- Cites all sources used in the analysis

Copernicus and the Universe

Nicolaus Copernicus was born Mikolaj Kopernik in Poland on February 19, 1473. He changed his name to a Latinized version while he was studying at the University of Krakow between 1491 and 1494. Copernicus' early studies included astronomy, Latin, math, geography, philosophy, Greek, and religious law.

Copernicus proposed a heliocentric system, meaning that it put the Sun at the center of the universe.

Copernicus was appointed as canon of Frauenburg Cathedral in Germany. He maintained the position for the rest of his life, despite never actually being ordained as a priest. Astronomy remained his passion.

The Shape of the Universe

In the 1400s, astronomy was still based mainly on the observations of the ancient Greek astronomer Ptolemy. Everyone assumed that the Earth was the center of the **universe** and that the Sun, Moon, and planets revolved around it. Ptolemy believed in an idea called the perfection of the heavens. This idea suggested that the orbits of the celestial bodies must be perfect, because they were part of the divine realm. That meant the orbits must be circular. However, this was not supported by observations of the planets' orbits. Today, scientists know that planetary orbits are elliptical or oval.

To explain the anomalies, Ptolemy came up with the idea of "epicycles." These were small circular movements he suggested the planets must make within their orbits as they traveled around Earth. Copernicus, however, realized that many of the mathematical problems inherent in Ptolemy's system would disappear if Earth moved around the Sun, rather than the other way around.

The Little Commentary

In 1514, Copernicus began distributing copies of a handwritten book. The book laid out the basic principles of a heliocentric, or Sun-centered, universe. The principles said that the center of the universe was not Earth, but a point near the Sun. The book also suggested that the universe was unimaginably large, and that the apparent rotation of the stars and seasonal movements of the Sun are caused by the rotation of Earth on its axis, and its movement around the Sun. Finally, Copernicus said that the movement of Earth influences astronomers' observations of the movements made by other planets.

The book became known as the "Little Commentary." It contained no detailed mathematics, and Copernicus did not even put his name to it. He was saving the details for his "larger work." Copernicus probably began writing that book, *De Revolutionibus Orbium Coelestium*, meaning "On the Revolutions of the Heavenly Orbs," in 1506. He did not complete it until 1530. He was conscious of the implications for the Catholic Church, which taught that Earth was the center of God's creation, so he allowed the manuscript to be read only by a few fellow scientists.

It was Copernicus' student, a German astronomer and mathematician named Rheticus, who persuaded him to publish *De Revolutionibus*. By the time the book was published, however, Copernicus was on his deathbed.

Appeal to the Pope

Copernicus knew his groundbreaking work *Revolutionibus Orbium Coelestium* (On the Revolutions of the Celestial Spheres) would be controversial, so he included a preface addressed to Pope Paul III. Copernicus explained that he was encouraged to publish the book by Cardinal Schonberg of Capua and other senior members of the Catholic Church. Copernicus tells the pope that he realizes that the work breaks new ground, but that he believes the truth is all important. He asks Paul to help protect him against the criticism that he knows his work will inevitably attract. Copernicus went on to say that those who believe Earth is at the center of the universe are forced to make many compromises in their calculations. On the other hand, his explanation that the Sun is at the center makes all the math work out perfectly. In spite of Copernicus' appeal to the pope, it took centuries for the Catholic Church to accept his theory.

ACTIVITIES

Document

English Translation of The Little Commentary

Examine this English translation of Copernicus' Little Commentary.

1. Why does Copernicus not provide detailed mathematical proofs of his ideas in this book? Summarize where Copernicus' view of the universe differs from our own.
2. Explain what Copernicus means when he states that "the Earth has, then, more than one motion." Describe what Copernicus calls "declination."

Weblink

Who Was Nicolaus Copernicus?

Assess this life of Nicolaus Copernicus.

1. Why did Copernicus worry that his theories would be scorned? Why did religious some religious leaders try to discredit the notion that Earth could be capable of motion?
2. Why did Galileo Galilei eventually support Copernicus and his theory of heliocentrism? Explain Galilei's reasoning.

RUBRIC

Creating a Timeline

Students will explore the development of gunpowder weapons and create a timeline to present their research on scientific events connected to this topic. An exemplary timeline will meet the following criteria.

- Includes the most significant events pertaining to the topic to be compared and analyzed
- Includes interesting events
- Uses accurate information for all events, including date, location, and major details
- Orders the events in a chronological sequence
- Describes each event with accurate, vivid, and specific details
- Presents the topic from three or more perspectives
- Inspires the reader to ask thoughtful questions regarding the events and perspectives presented in the timeline
- Uses correct spelling, grammar, and punctuation
- Presents the timeline in a visually attractive and striking manner
- Presents the timeline in a neat, organized manner that is logical and easy to follow
- Uses creativity to present the timeline in an engaging manner
- Effectively communicates historical information relating to the topic
- Supports each event with reliable sources
- Includes a correctly formatted bibliography of all sources used to create the timeline

The Age of Gunpowder

Gunpowder is a mixture of charcoal, sulfur, and saltpeter, or potassium nitrate. When mixed in the correct proportions, it burns rapidly. The hot gases produced expand and explode with a loud bang. If burned at the closed end of an open-ended tube, the expanding hot gases will push out a ball or bullet.

Cannon

First use: China, 1280s

Projectile: Solid shot or exploding shell

Construction: Solid cast metal or bundles of rods hooped together

Major innovation: Wheeled gun carriage

Major effect: Reduced importance of stone castles in warfare

Weakness: Prone to explode during use, killing the gunners

Harquebus

First use: Spain, mid-1400s

Projectile: Solid shot

Construction: Tube of iron or brass

Major innovation: Touchhole used to ignite gunpowder moved from the top to the side of the weapon, lighted cord used to ignite the powder

Major effect: Made defensive armor less effective on the battlefield

Weakness: Inaccurate and unwieldy

This is the principle of the cannon and all firearms. Gunpowder was used in fireworks in China in the 1100s. In about 1220, the Chinese made bombs that shattered on explosion. The gunpowder cannon appeared in the late 1280s, when the Chinese used what they called “erupters” to fire stones at the enemy.

Matchlock Musket

First use: Spain, 1530s

Projectile: Solid shot

Construction: Tube of iron or brass

Major innovation: Fired by resting on a forked post

Major effect: More accurate than the harquebus. Could be carried into battle and used to fire in volleys

Weakness: Heavy to carry and useless in wet weather, when it did not spark so could not fire

Flintlock Musket

First use: France, 1660s

Projectile: Solid shot

Construction: Tube of iron

Major innovation: Gunpowder ignited by flint striking steel

Major effect: Made pistols easier to carry on horseback

Weakness: Very inaccurate at ranges longer than 100 yards (100 m)

More

The Age of Gunpowder

Review the four types of early gunpowder weapon: cannon, harquebus, matchlock musket, flintlock musket. Research further online.

1. Summarize why the flintlock musket was an improvement over the matchlock. Why was the flintlock accurate only to 100 yards (91 meters) at most?
2. Describe the problems of firing flintlocks in rain. Why were flintlocks most effective when used by a line of infantry firing volleys?

RUBRIC

Researching for a Writing Assignment

Students will complete a thorough research process to prepare for a writing assignment on why Christopher Columbus believed the world was round, and organize their research in a logical manner that supports their writing. An exemplary research process will meet the following criteria.

- Creates a goal for the research, based on the topic and working thesis
- Creates specific, thoughtful, and inventive research questions that are relevant to the topic of the writing assignment
- Produces a list of categories, key words, and related ideas to effectively assist in researching
- Uses high-quality sources that pertain to the topic and come in a variety of formats, such as books, journals, primary sources, websites, and databases
- Uses sources that provide balanced research and various perspectives of the topic in question
- Takes notes to highlight the key facts and ideas in order to answer all research questions
- Extracts relevant, detailed information from the sources
- Writes notes in the student's own words
- Organizes the research notes in a clear and concise manner
- Analyzes the information and produces ideas and points to support the working thesis
- Uses an effective and suitable format to present all research
- Properly cites all sources used
- Uses quotations properly and ethically

Voyages of Discovery

The square-sailed ships used in northern Europe in the Middle Ages, and the oar-powered galleys used in the Mediterranean, were not reliable enough for sailing in the Atlantic Ocean. Then, in about 1445, Portuguese shipbuilders developed a new type of vessel called a caravel. It had two or three masts with one square sail and a set of triangular sails behind these.

The extra sails on the caravel gave the ship better maneuverability. Caravels enabled longer ocean journeys to take place. Portuguese sailors moved out into the Atlantic. In 1487, the Portuguese **navigator** Bartholomew Diaz sailed down the west coast of Africa. A storm drove him south. When he turned north, he rounded the southern tip of the continent, the Cape of Good Hope. Diaz came ashore on the east coast of Africa in 1488.

In 1498, another Portuguese navigator, Vasco da Gama, followed Diaz's earlier route. He continued on up the coast of East Africa. Then, he sailed across the Indian Ocean. Da Gama made landfall in India. He established a new trade route to India and Asia and later, on a second voyage in 1502, he reached the Spice Islands, or Moluccas. The islands were the source of valuable spices.

The caravel had a wide, relatively shallow hull. This helped it remain stable on the open oceans.

ACTIVITIES

Christopher Columbus landed on Hispaniola on October 12, 1492. He was convinced he had reached East Asia.

Weblink

The Caravel

Review the weblink on the caravel.

1. Summarize the reasons why the caravel was so versatile. What was the importance of the lateen sail?
2. Describe the most important duties of the crewmen of a caravel. What navigation aids would a caravel have carried?

Discovering America

Meanwhile, in 1492, a navigator from Genoa in Italy persuaded the king and queen of Spain to fund an expedition to try to find a westerly route to India by crossing the Atlantic Ocean. The navigator was Christopher Columbus, and his three ships were the caravels *Santa Maria*, *Niña*, and *Pinta*. Instead of reaching Asia, Columbus landed in the present-day Bahamas, off the east coast of America. He returned home in 1493, leaving a colony of 39 men on the island he named Hispaniola, now known as Haiti. Columbus made a second and third voyage, from 1493 to 1495, and from 1498 to 1500. On his second journey, he landed in Central America and discovered many Caribbean islands. On the third voyage, Columbus landed in Trinidad, and then in South America. On a final voyage, he explored the Gulf of Mexico.

In fall 1519, Ferdinand Magellan set out with 265 men and five ships to sail around South America. His fleet crossed the Atlantic and around the tip of South America. He lost four ships in storms crossing the Pacific Ocean. Magellan was killed in 1521, by local people in the Philippines. In 1522, one ship and just 20 men returned to Spain. These sailors had become the first people to **circumnavigate** the globe.

RUBRIC

Presentation on a Famous Sailing Vessel

Create a PowerPoint presentation about a famous sailing vessel used during the European voyages of exploration.
An exemplary PowerPoint presentation will meet the following criteria.

- Includes information about the function and style highlights of the vessel
- Describes the main materials used and explains the reason for their selection
- Explains any other considerations that the vessel's design took into account
- Appropriate photographs or illustrations of the vessel are included in the presentation and photographers are credited
- The speaker delivers the message in a confident, poised, enthusiastic fashion
- The volume and rate varies to add emphasis and interest
- Pronunciation and enunciation are very clear
- The speaker exhibits very few filler words, such as "ahs," "uhms," or "you knows"
- The speaker helps the listener understand the sequence and relationships of ideas by using organizational aids such as announcing the topic, previewing the organization, using transitions, and summarizing
- Very original presentation of material; captures the audience's attention
- Appropriate use of visual aids to add interest and clarify concepts
- Within two minutes of allotted time.

Map of Exploration

In the fifteenth and sixteenth centuries, technical developments in shipbuilding enabled European sailors to make more ambitious voyages across the open oceans. The developments included the use of triangular, or lateen, sails and better methods of navigation, such as the magnetic compass. Portuguese sailors moved down the coast of Africa and rounded the Cape of Good Hope at the continent's southern tip. From there, they crossed the Indian Ocean to India, where they could obtain valuable spices. The Spanish monarchy financed westward voyages by Christopher Columbus. Although Columbus failed to find the route to Asia he was hoping for, his arrival in the "New World" of the Americas had equally momentous consequences. It began a transatlantic exchange of animals, plants, people, religions, and ideas that continues today.

LEGEND

N

- Country
- Ocean
- Major voyage of discovery
- Diaz, 1487–1488
- Columbus, 1492–1493
- da Gama, 1497–1499
- Magellan, 1519–1522

0 — 2,000 miles
0 — 4,000 kilometers

THE BAHAMAS

When Columbus reached the Bahamas in 1492, he believed he had reached the "Indies" of East Asia. The islands are part of the region still known as the West Indies. They became a base from which Spain built up an empire in South, Central, and North America.

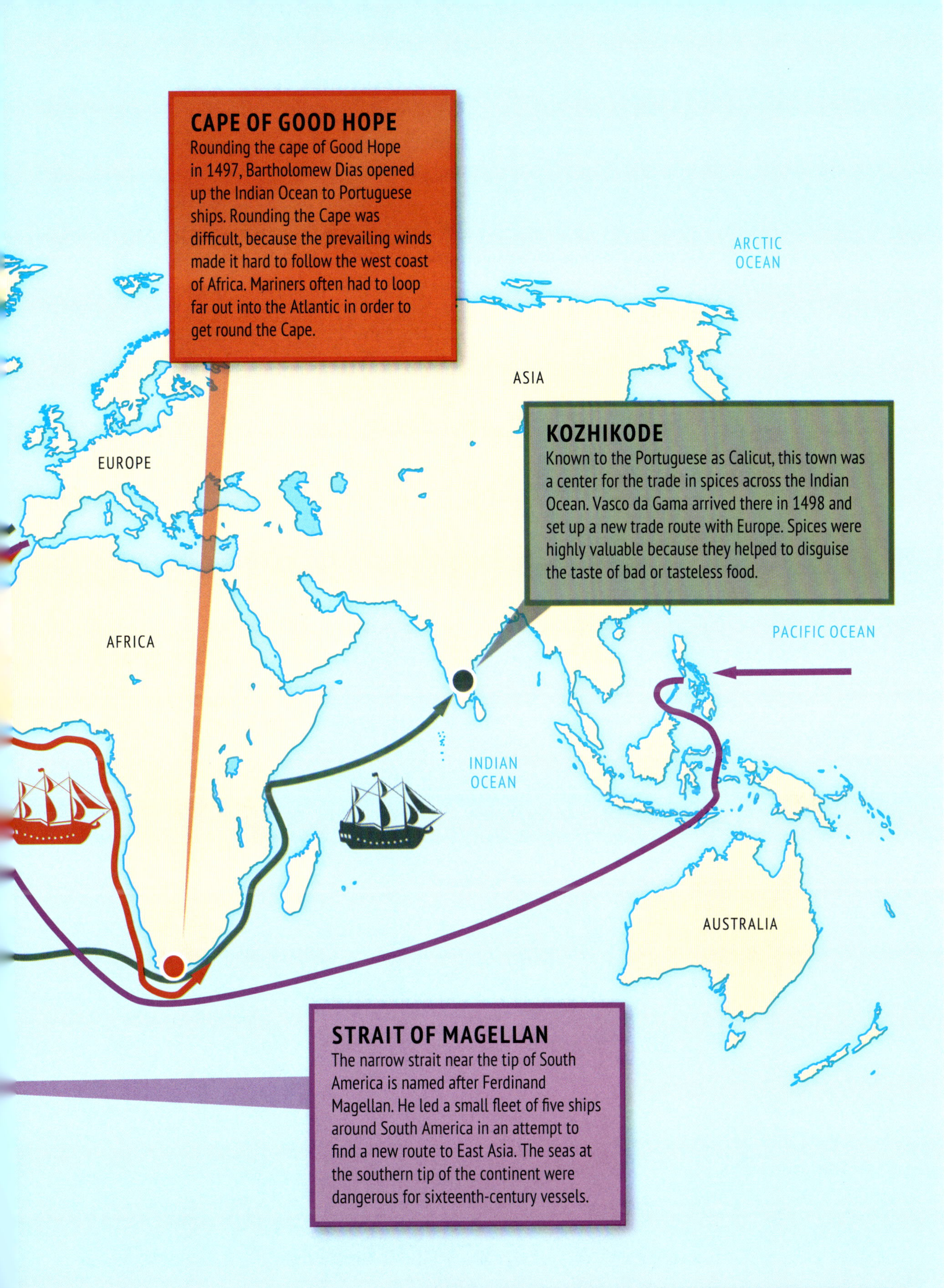

ACTIVITIES

Google Maps

Map of Exploration

Examine the map of the major voyages of discovery during the age of exploration.

1. Why did Portuguese vessels sail so far out into the Atlantic before they rounded the Cape of Good Hope? Before the Portuguese rounded the Cape of Good Hope, what had been the route by which spices from India reached Europe?
2. Summarize the obstacles that Portuguese found in establishing trade across the Indian Ocean. Research the Treaty of Tordesillas between Spain and Portugal, and explain its importance.
3. Why did Columbus believe that he had arrived off the coast of China when he arrived in the Bahamas? Why were his calculations so wrong?

CAPE OF GOOD HOPE

Rounding the cape of Good Hope in 1497, Bartholomew Dias opened up the Indian Ocean to Portuguese ships. Rounding the Cape was difficult, because the prevailing winds made it hard to follow the west coast of Africa. Mariners often had to loop far out into the Atlantic in order to get round the Cape.

KOZHIKODE

Known to the Portuguese as Calicut, this town was a center for the trade in spices across the Indian Ocean. Vasco da Gama arrived there in 1498 and set up a new trade route with Europe. Spices were highly valuable because they helped to disguise the taste of bad or tasteless food.

STRAIT OF MAGELLAN

The narrow strait near the tip of South America is named after Ferdinand Magellan. He led a small fleet of five ships around South America in an attempt to find a new route to East Asia. The seas at the southern tip of the continent were dangerous for sixteenth-century vessels.

Sailing Ships

In medieval Europe, sails were square or rectangular sheets of canvas attached to a single mast. They were used in addition to oars to push boats along. Sails were used only when the wind was blowing in the direction the sailor wished to travel.

By the third century AD, in the Arabian Sea, square sails were replaced by triangular sails. These sails allowed ships to sail almost directly into the wind. At this time, the most advanced ships were built in East Asia. In China, multimasted ships called junks carried sails that were square at the bottom and triangular at the top. Junks were in use on China's rivers as early as the sixth century.

Before the 1400s century, ships in northern Europe were "clinker built." This meant that their hulls had overlapping planks, rather than being edge to edge. They had a hinged **rudder** for steering. In the Mediterranean, many ships were galleys, or narrow ships powered by oars. By about 1200, galleys were replaced by ships with two masts and two sails. These caravels were faster than clinker-built ships. Fighting platforms known as castles were often built in the front and back of ships.

New Vessels in Europe

By the late 1400s, shipbuilders in western Europe were familiar with all sorts of ships. They combined the best features of different technologies. Some caravels were converted from **lateen** riggers to square riggers.

Cannons along the sides of caravels and caracks created efficient warships.

ACTIVITIES

Hull design

In clinker-built ships, the hull was supported internally by the addition of wooden ribs. The design originated before the invention of the saw, when planks were cut using a bladed hand tool called an adz. The result was a rough cut that meant it was not possible to abut planks directly. The clinker-built style placed a natural limit on the size of the ship. If a ship was over about 100 feet (30 m) long, it became impossible for the overlapping planks to be joined tightly enough. Early Mediterranean ships, on the other hand, were built with square-cut planks. The planks were fitted to a prefabricated frame. These carvel-built ships were not as watertight as clinker-built ones, but they were much lighter and could be built to a larger size.

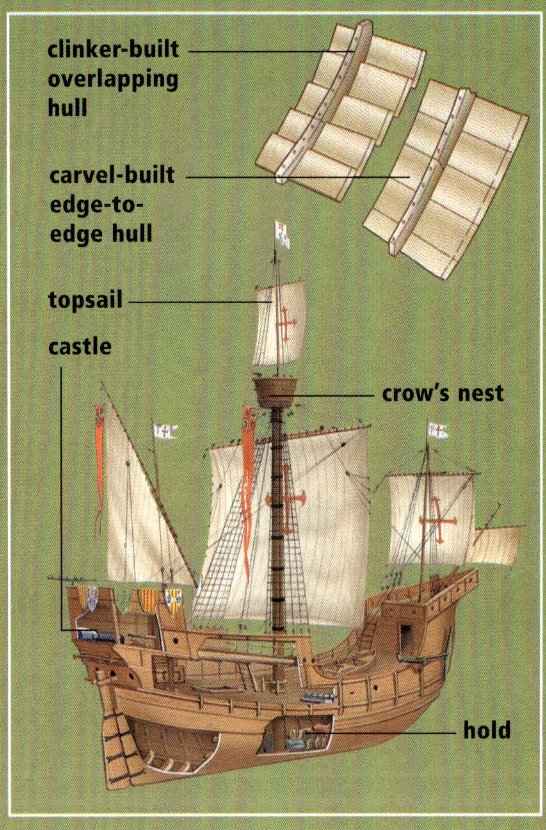

These converted caravels included the *Santa Maria*, flagship of the transatlantic explorer Christopher Columbus. The definitive exploration vessel was the carrack. This was a carvel-built hull with a hinged stern rudder. It had a large castle built into the rounded stern, a main mast bearing a square sail, and a second "mizzen" mast with a triangular sail in back of the ship. A third mast was added later toward the front of the ship. This mast carried a triangular foresail used mainly for steering. In later carracks, this foresail was much larger, and added significantly to the speed of the ship.

Generating Speed

Speed was directly related to the area of sail a ship carried. By the late 1400s, carracks carried additional topsails on their main and foremasts. Some carried a third sail above the main topsail. A fourth mast was added to the largest carracks in the sixteenth century. Carracks were dangerous places, with a web of rigging under enormous tension from the canvas. Carracks were used for exploration and for war. By the 1500s, they were being built large enough to carry cannons, and were robust enough to withstand the massive recoil when the cannons were fired.

Transparency

Hull Design

Examine the construction of a ship's hull.

1. Describe the limitations of clinker-built vessels in the middle ages. Why would explorers have wanted to set sail in larger vessels?
2. Explain the importance of topsails. How would carracks have coped with the recoil of cannons? Describe the process.

Weblink

Development of Sailing Ships

Examine the weblink about the development of sailing vessels.

1. Did Chinese junk design have any effect on European sailing vessels? Why did caravels lose some lateen sails in the "redonda" configuration?
2. Explain any major differences between merchant ships and warships in the 1500s. Compare the distances a ship could travel in a single day with the speed of land transport in the 1500s.

Early Chinese compasses used a magnetized ladle, or spoon that turned on a flat base.

The Magnetic Compass

The history of the compass is intertwined with magnetism. Like a magnet, Earth's magnetic field has two poles, north and south. A magnetized object, such as a lodestone or compass needle, tries to align itself to Earth's magnetic field. By the first century AD in China, lodestones were being used in devices called south-pointers.

Magnetized Needles

During the eighth century, the lodestone in Chinese compasses was replaced by a magnetized iron needle. The needle was magnetized by laying it along the magnetic axis of a good lodestone. In 1086, the Chinese scientist Shen Kua gave the first clear description of a magnetic compass used for navigation. The first description of a compass being used at sea was written in China in 1117.

It was not until the age of European exploration in the 1400s and 1500s that the compass became a reliable navigational aid. As with other innovations from China, it was probably brought to the West by the Arabs. Before that, European travelers used the Sun or the Pole Star to show them north and south. Such guides only worked with clear skies, however. They were useless in bad weather. The first written reference to a magnetic compass in the West was published in 1180 by the English scholar and cleric Alexander Neckam.

From East to West

Early European compasses used a magnetized needle thrust perpendicularly through a straw that floated upright in a dish of water. The device provided a reasonably accurate fix on north and south, but it was not portable or convenient for sea travel. By 1250, the needle was mounted on a pivot and hovered beneath a circular card marked with the cardinal directions. When the needle moved, so did the card.

The laws governing the behavior of magnets, and therefore of the compass, were first described by the French scientist and soldier Petrus Peregrinus in 1269. He described magnetic poles and developed a compass dial. The new dial allowed the compass needle to be used to indicate directions to within a single degree of arc.

Further Modifications

Refinements in compass technology included mounting the needle and dial in a box. These containers were made of material such as wood or ivory that did not interfere with the magnetic forces. Later models were made from brass.

In the 1500s, marine compasses were mounted on bearings. These "gimbals" kept the compass level, despite the rolling of the ship.

Sailors came to rely on the compass. In 1594, English philosopher Francis Bacon called the "needle" one of the three most important advances in the civilized world. The others were gunpowder and the printing press. Each year, thousands of sailors risked their lives setting sail on courses indicated by nothing more than a quivering shard of iron.

Portable compasses were ornately carved from materials such as ivory. They were often protected by a lid.

Document

The Letter of Petrus Peregrinus on the Magnet, 1269 AD

Review the letter of Peregrinus.

1. Summarize Peregrinus' description of the qualities of a good lodestone. Explain the process whereby lodestone magnetizes iron.
2. Describe the importance of the dial within a box that Peregrinus developed. What would be a bad material for constructing the box?

First Hand

Descriptions and primary source accounts of the early use of the Magnetic Compass in China.

Examine the website on the development of the magnetic compass.

1. Describe the importance of lodestone in the development of the magnetic compass in China. Why was the iron "fish" heated before it was put into water?
2. What method of navigation did the magnetic compass supplement or replace for Chinese navigators? Describe the difference between magnetic north and true north.

RUBRIC

Create a Poster

Create a poster on the development of printing using movable type from 500 to 1700. An exemplary poster will meet the following criteria.

- The poster has a title that suggests the chosen topic or theme
- The poster presents relevant and accurate information about the topic or theme
- The format of the poster is appropriate to the content, purpose, and audience that it was designed for
- Visuals such as pictures, photographs, charts, tables, scientific drawings, diagrams add to the effectiveness of the poster
- The poster is well organized, and the poster elements work well together
- The use of appropriate graphic design tools, space, color, texture, and shape effectively creates an aesthetically pleasing product
- The poster draws attention
- Language chosen for the poster is accurate, informative, and concise

Measuring Time

The shadow clock was used in Egypt by about 3500 BC. It was a vertical stick, which cast a shadow as the Sun moved. At night, the Egyptians told time with a clepsydra. This was a vessel from which water dripped out through a hole. By the eighth century BC, the shadow clock had evolved into the sundial.

Water Clocks

When invented: 700s

Where invented: China

Inventor: Liang Ling-Zan and Yi-Xing

Advantages: Functioned as a calendar as well as a clock

Drawbacks: Large, difficult to assemble, not easily portable

Mechanical Clocks

When invented: Late 900s

Where invented: France

Inventor: Gerbert of Aurillac

Advantages: Told time in towns by regular sounding of the hours by bells

Drawbacks: Large and complex

ACTIVITIES

Sand clocks also date from ancient times. The commonest type was the hourglass. It took one hour for dry sand to run through the narrow neck from the upper section to the lower section. In the medieval period, people began to tell the time using new, mechanical methods that predate today's clocks.

Pocket Watches

When invented: 1542

Where invented: Germany

Inventor: Peter Henlein

Advantages: Portable

Drawbacks: Had to be created by skilled watchmaker. Lacked hands, simply striking the hours

Pendulum Clocks

When invented: 1656

Where invented: Holland

Inventor: Christiaan Huygens

Advantages: Was the first timepiece to have both a face and two hands, like a modern clock

Drawbacks: Could only be created and maintained by a skilled watchmaker

More

Measuring Time

Review the information on the pendulum clock. Research online.

1. Why was the first pendulum clock not built by the man who devised it? Describe the role of the anchor in a pendulum clock.
2. Explain how the pendulum clock was powered. Describe other Renaissance technologies that relied on accurate gearing mechanisms.

The lack of copyright laws allowed printers simply to copy the books of their rivals. This encouraged the spread of ideas.

Development of the Printing Press

Printing originated in China. In about the ninth century, Chinese printers made paper money and books. Each page of characters was carved from a single block of wood to make a printing "plate." By 1045, the Chinese printer Bi Sheng had invented movable type made from baked clay. Within 10 years, he was printing books with it. The Chinese language has thousands of different characters. In 1313, the printer Wang Chen used more than 50,000 movable wooden characters to print his *Treatise on Agriculture*. Printing from cast-metal type began in Korea in the 1390s. In 1403, King Taejong authorized the casting of metal type in bronze.

In 1438, the Dutch printer Laurens Koster of Haarlem, in the Netherlands, is thought to have used movable wooden blocks for printing. Metal type was first used in Europe by the German inventor Johannes Gutenberg in the 1440s. Gutenberg brought together different ideas. He made copper molds in which to cast the type using a low-melting lead alloy. He also introduced a special oil-based printing ink. Most importantly, Gutenberg used a printing press to squeeze the paper against the inked printing plates. He adapted the screw press previously used for crushing the juice out of grapes to make wine.

The First Printed Books

Gutenberg set up his first printing press in about 1442 in Strasbourg, France. In about 1450, however, he returned home to Mainz, in Germany.

He established a printing press using money put up by the businessman Johann Fust and a fellow printer named Peter Schöffer. Gutenberg's first production was the world's first book ever to be printed using movable metal type. It was a Latin Bible, which he produced in 1455 with a new partner named Konrad Humery.

The first printed book in Europe to carry the name of its printer was a psalter, or book of psalms. It was produced in 1457 by Peter Schöffer. This book was also the first to be printed in two colors. In about 1475, Schöffer, who by then had set up in business on his own, began using steel dies to stamp out the copper molds for typecasting.

As details of the technology spread, printing presses began to appear in other parts of Europe. The first press in Italy, at Subiaco near Rome, was established in 1465. By 1470, the university in Paris had its own press for printing academic works.

Caxton Press

Metal-type printing was introduced into England by William Caxton. In 1474, Caxton was living in Bruges in Belgium, where he collaborated with the Flemish calligrapher Colard Mansion. Caxton became the first person to print a book in the English language. Caxton returned to England in 1476, and established a printing press in London the following year. In 1481, he published the first illustrated book in English.

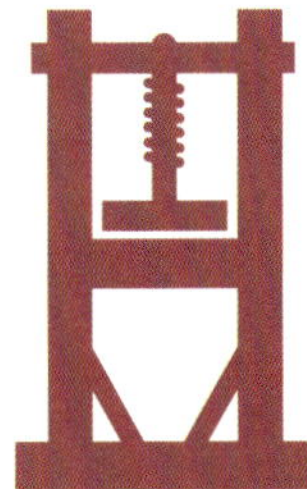

290

GUTENBERG BIBLE

Gutenberg used 290 master type slugs to print his Bible.

49

GUTENBERG BIBLE

Only 49 Gutenberg Bibles have survived until the present day. Of these, only nine retain their fifteenth-century bindings.

Where it is so that euery humayn Creature by the suffrance of our lord god is born & ordeigned to be subgette and thral vnto the stormes of fortune And so in diuerse & many sondry wyses man is perplexid with worldly aduersitees / Of the whiche I Antoine Wydeuille Erle Ryuyeres / lord Scales &c haue largely & in many different maners haue had my parte And of hem releued by thynfynyte grace & goodnes of our said lord thurgh the meane of the Mediatrice of Mercy / Whiche hath euidently to me knowen & vnderstonde hath compelled me to sette a parte alle ingratitude / And drof me by reson & conscience as fer as my wrecchednes wold suffyse to gyue therfore synguler louynges & thankes / And exorted me to dispose my recouerd lyf to his seruyce / in folowyng his lawes and comandements / And in satisfaccion & recompence of myn Inyquytees & fawtes before don / to seke & execute the werkes that myght be most acceptable to hym / And as fer as myn fraylnes wold suffre me I rested in that wylle & purpose Duryng that season I vnderstode the Jubylee & pardon to be at the holy Appostle Seynt James in Spayne whiche was the yere of grace a thousand. CCCC. lxxiij. Thenne I determyned me to take that voyage & shipped from southampton in the moneth of Juyll the said yere / And so sayled from thens til I come in to the Spaynyssh see there lackyng syght of alle londes / the wynde beyng good and the weder fayr / Thenne for a recreacion & a passyng of tyme I had delyte & axed to rede some good historye And amonge other ther was that season in my companye a worshipful gentylman callid lowys de Bretaylles / Whiche gretly delited

The first book printed in England was *The Sayings of the Philosophers*, a compilation of quotations from biblical and classical thinkers.

ACTIVITIES

Video

Gutenberg's Printing Process

Review the video on Gutenberg's typesetting process.

1. Why is it unclear which precise method Gutenberg used for creating type? Compare the advantages of sand and copper as the molds into which to pour the lead alloy for the type.
2. Why were the lines of Gutenberg's Bible so close together? Why would an oil-based ink be better than a water-based ink?

Weblink

William Caxton

Examine the weblink on Caxton's printing career.

1. Caxton translated into English many of the books he printed. Why would this be unusual nowadays? Why was proofreading so important to the printing process in Caxton's time?
2. Estimate how many sheets of printed paper Caxton's printing machine could produce in an hour. Explain the importance of woodcuts to illustrate books.

RUBRIC

You Decide

English philosopher Francis Bacon wrote that there were three critical inventions of the late middle ages: the magnetic compass, gunpowder, and the printing press. Construct an argument that puts these in order of importance. An exemplary argument will meet the following criteria:

- Provides background on the topic within the introduction
- Introduction is logical and provides accurate scientific information
- Alternative opinions are explained, and are related to the controversy of the topic
- Research is explained, including critiques of websites
- Scientific information is accurate. All relevant pieces of evidence are analyzed
- Well-supported stance is justified by analysis
- Explanation of stance incorporates and explains personal opinions, as well as reflects on opinions that changed throughout the research process
- Usefulness and credibility of websites is discussed
- More than four websites are consulted, and sources are properly cited
- Free of grammatical and spelling errors

Timeline of Science Discoveries

The medieval period and the Renaissance saw many discoveries being made around the world. These are some of the most important breakthroughs. They cover a wide range of fields of science.

	0–300	300–550	550–800	800–1000	1000–1250
Technology	**100** The wheelbarrow appears in China. **226** A 14-mile (22-km) aqueduct is completed to bring water to Rome.	**350** A water-powered sawmill is built in France for cutting marble. **510** Craftsmen build a chiming waterclock in Palestine, in the Middle East.	**680** The Dutch build large earthen dams, or dikes, to protect their low-lying land from floods. **748** The first printed newspaper appears in Beijing.	**800** The use of blast furnaces for smelting iron spreads across Europe. **868** The earliest surviving printed book is created in China.	**1150** The first papermill in Europe is built in Valencia in Spain. **1180** The first stern-mounted rudders are used to steer boats in Europe.
Physical/Life Sciences	**175** The Greek physician Galen begins feeling the pulse as part of diagnosis. His writings will become central to medical practice for over 1,000 years.	**512** Herbalists in Constantinople produce an illustrated book of herbs by the ancient Greek, Dioscorides. The book lays the basis of medicine in the Middle Ages.	**770** The Arab scholar known in the West as Geber describes how to create nitric acid and other chemicals.	**900** Arab chemists distill wine to make strong alcohol. **980** One of the world's first hospitals opens in Baghdad. It has 24 physicians.	**1000** The Persian philosopher Avicenna writes his *Canon of Medicine*. The book becomes a standard work for centuries, and will be translated into Latin in 1135.
Astronomy/Math	**150** Greek astronomer Ptolemy compiles his *Almagest*. This will become the standard work on astronomy until the Renaissance in Europe.	**369** Chinese astronomers observe a supernova, or exploding star. The event lasts for five months.	**610** Indian mathematicians begin using base 10 for their number system. **774** Arab mathematicians translate Hindi mathematical works into Arabic.	**876** The zero appears as a symbol in mathematical calculations in Gwalior, India.	**1175** Gerhard of Cremona makes the first Latin translation of Ptolemy's *Almagest*. **1202** Leonardo Fibonacci devises the sequence of numbers named for him.

ACTIVITIES

1250–1400	1400–1530	1530–1565	1565–1600	1600–1625
1228 Chinese engineers build "erupters," the first cannons. **1335** The Italian clockmaker Guglielmo Zelandino makes a striking clock for a tower in Milan.	**1442** Johannes Gutenberg sets up a printing press in Germany that uses movable type. **1453** Ottoman troops use a huge cannon in the victorious siege of Constantinople.	**1551** English mathematician Leonard Digges invents the theodolite for measuring angles during surveying	**1590** Dutchman Zacharias Jansen invents a compound microscope that uses two lenses. **1592** Italian scientist Galileo Galilei makes an air-filled thermometer.	**1608** Dutch inventor Hans Lippershey makes a refracting telescope with two lenses. **1622** William Oughtred invents the slide rule for calculations.
1267 The English scientist Roger Bacon suggests that magnifying glasses could help those with weak sight.	**1525** The Swiss alchemist Paracelsus publishes his *Great Surgery Book*, which disagrees with some of the teachings of Galen.	**1556** The German mineralogist Georgius Agricola describes the formation of minerals and how they are mined. He also describes extracting metals from ores.	**1582** Galileo Galilei discovers that a pendulum swings at a constant period. **1600** English scientist William Gilbert describes the magnetic properties of Earth.	**1620** The English philosopher Francis Bacon advocates the scientific method, using experiment to test theories.
1395 Chinese astronomers calculate the length of the solar year as 365.25 days. The accurate value is 365.242 days.	**1425** Nicholas of Cusa suggests that Earth revolves around the Sun. **1435** Italian architect Leon Alberti works out the scientific laws of perspective.	**1543** Publication of Copernicus' *De Revolutionibus Orbium Coelestium*, which proves Earth orbits the Sun.	**1569** Flemish cartographer Gerardus Mercator introduces the Mercator map projection. **1594** The Scottish mathematician John Napier devises logarithms.	**1609** German astronomer Johannes Kepler draws up his first two laws of planetary motion.

Transparency

Timeline

Analyze key events in the technology of the Medieval Period and the Renaissance.

1. Describe the inventions that were designed to increase control of water. Explain how the medieval blast furnace was an advance on previous furnaces.
2. Describe the technological background to the development of microscopes and telescopes. Why might Archimedes have approved of the principles behind the invention of the wheelbarrow?

Quiz

1 Where was the world's first printed book created?

2 Where was zero invented as a tool for math?

3 What was the House of Wisdom?

4 Who sailed across the Atlantic in dragon ships?

5 What did Leonardo Fibonacci explain in his *Book of Calculation* of 1202?

6 What was the *Little Commentary* of 1514?

7 What is produced by mixing charcoal, sulfur, and saltpeter?

8 In 1519, who set out on a voyage that eventually went round the world?

9 What are carracks and caravels?

10 What was Gutenberg's printing press developed from?

ANSWERS

1. In China, in 868 **2.** In India, in 878 **3.** An academy in Baghdad that included an astronomical observatory **4.** The Vikings, who reached North America in about 1000 **5.** How to use Arabic numerals **6.** Copernicus' digest of his theory that Earth moves round the Sun **7.** Gunpowder **8.** Ferdinand Magellan **9.** Sailing ships used in European voyages of exploration in the 1400s and 1500s **10.** The screw press used for crushing grapes for wine

Study the Sources

The history of science is a complicated subject. Historians must be able to understand scientific processes as well as the ways in which history changes because of social, economic, political, or military pressures and opportunities. Adding to the difficulty, the people who recorded advances in the past often did not understand what was actually happening in the scientific developments they were describing.

Consider a major theme discussed in this book. Topics you might choose could be papermaking, gunpowder and guns, or waterwheels or windmills.

Use the internet to find at least two descriptions and at least two images of the topic. Try to find images from China and Arabia as well as European sources. Note how people from different cultures or different centuries portrayed different aspects as being important.

Compare the descriptions and images you find with this book. How accurate do you think the sources are in their scientific descriptions? Do the words or images reflect the science behind what is happening? Or do you feel the artists or writers do not understand what they are looking at?

Key Words

alchemy: an ancient pseudoscience focused on the attempt to change base metals into gold

algebra: the branch of mathematics that studies the properties of mathematical structures, and in which unknown quantities are denoted by letters

anchor escapement: a clock mechanism that allows much smaller arcs of swing of a pendulum than in earlier clocks

astronomers: people who study objects outside Earth's atmosphere

circumnavigate: to travel all around an area by boat or ship, as around Earth

counterweight: something heavy placed at one end of a balance to make it easier to raise a weight at the other end

double-entry bookkeeping: an accounting technique that records each transaction as both a credit and a debit

escapement: in clocks and watches, a mechanism that controls the gradual release of energy from a falling weight or coiled spring

geometry: the branch of mathematics that deals with the properties, measurement, and relationships of points, lines, angles, surfaces, and solids

horsepower: a unit of power defined as the amount of power that can move a 550-pound object 1 foot in a second of time

lateen: a triangular sail rigged so that the sail lies along the axis of the vessel, allowing it to navigate against the prevailing wind

magnetic: in navigation, this describes an object that turns to point to Earth's north and south poles

movable type: small blocks of wood or metal carved with letters or numbers for printing. After a page has been printed, the blocks can be disassembled and reused to print another page.

navigator: the person who directs the course of a ship

philosopher: someone who thinks in a systematic way about complex questions relating to life and existence

printing press: a machine that transfers lettering or images, by contact with various forms of inked surface, onto paper or similar material

rudder: a vertically hinged plate mounted at the stern of a ship for directing its course

silk: the material made from the very fine, soft, lustrous fiber produced by a silkworm

slide rule: a device consisting of two logarithmically scaled rules mounted to slide along each other to help in calculations

universe: the whole of space, time, and everything in it

Index

LIGHTBOX

SUPPLEMENTARY RESOURCES

Click on the plus icon found in the bottom left corner of each spread to open additional teacher resources.

- Download and print the book's quizzes and activities
- Access curriculum correlations
- Explore additional web applications that enhance the Lightbox experience

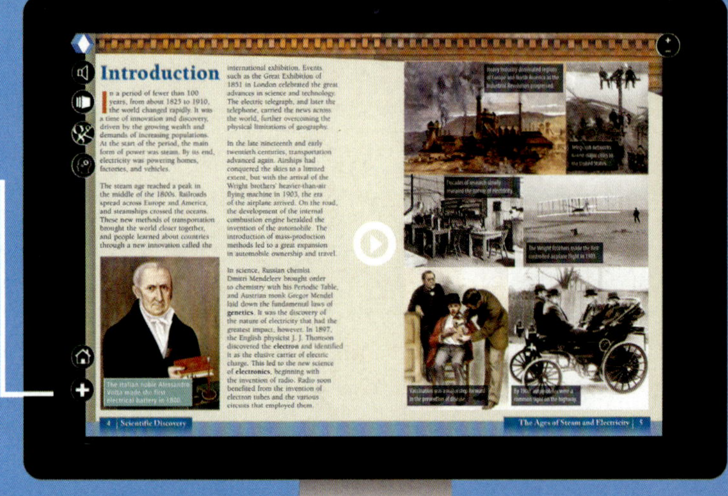

LIGHTBOX DIGITAL TITLES
Packed full of integrated media

VIDEOS

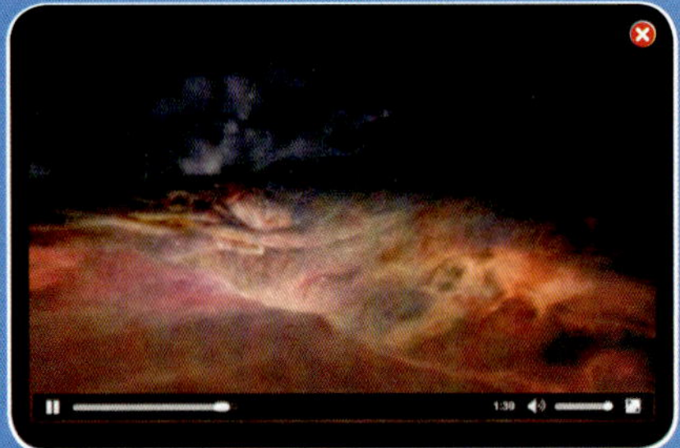

INTERACTIVE MAPS

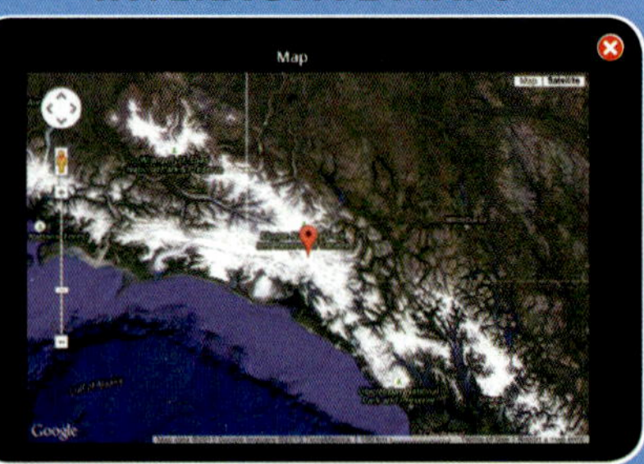

WEBLINKS

SLIDESHOWS

QUIZZES

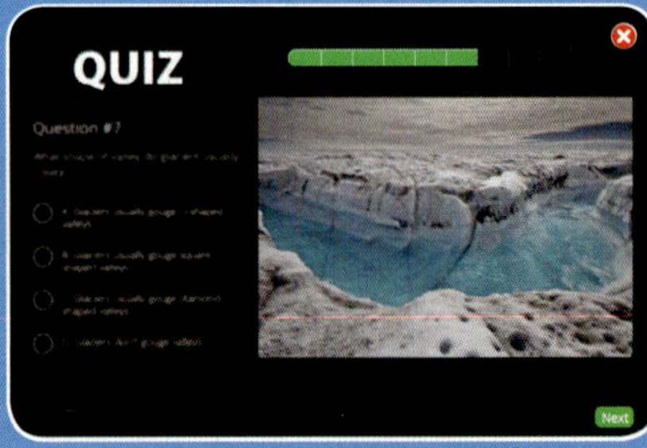

OPTIMIZED FOR
- ✓ TABLETS
- ✓ WHITEBOARDS
- ✓ COMPUTERS
- ✓ AND MUCH MORE!

Published by Smartbook Media Inc.
350 5th Avenue, 59th Floor New York, NY 10118
Website: www.openlightbox.com

First published by Brown Bear Books in 2009

Library of Congress Control Number: 2018941506

ISBN 978-1-5105-3763-7 (hardcover)
ISBN 978-1-5105-3764-4 (multi-user eBook)

Printed in Brainerd, Minnesota, United States
1 2 3 4 5 6 7 8 9 0 22 21 20 19 18

072018
121217

Project Coordinator: Heather Kissock
Art Director: Ana María Vidal

Every reasonable effort has been made to trace ownership and to obtain permission to reprint copyright material. The publisher would be pleased to have any errors or omissions brought to its attention so that they may be corrected in subsequent printings.

The publisher acknowledges Getty Images, Alamy, Newscom, iStock, Shutterstock, and Wikimedia as its primary image suppliers for this title.